# Riseley

# Our Village

*"Riseley – Our Village" is proudly
dedicated to the memory of
Michael Ives who died
before the publication of the
book he inspired.*

# Riseley

# Our Village

Written and published by Riseley Historical Society

Edited by Sue Davies

Riseley – Our Village
Copyright © Riseley Historical Society 2000

All Rights Reserved

No part of this book may be reproduced in any form, by photocopying or by any electronic or mechanical means, including information storage or retrieval systems, without the permission in writing from the copyright owner and publisher of this book

ISBN 0-9539263-0-3

First published November 2000 by Riseley Historical Society

Printed in Great Britain by Newnorth Print Limited

# Contents

| | Page |
|---|---|
| List of Illustrations | viii |
| Riseley Historical Society | xiii |
| Map of Riseley | xiv |
| Foreword – John Ashworth, British Library | xv |
| Clearing in the Brushwood | 1 |
| Did you know that . . . | 10 |
| All Saints Church – The People and their Building | 11 |
|     The Church Vestry | 15 |
|     Free Seats for All | 20 |
|     The Phoney Curate | 22 |
|     Major Re-ordering in the Church | 23 |
|     A New Era | 25 |
|     Facing the Future | 28 |
| Did you know that . . . | 32 |
| The Moravians, Methodists and Baptists | 33 |
|     The Moravian Church | 33 |
|     The Methodist Church | 36 |
|     The Particular or Strict Baptists | 42 |
| Did you know that . . . | 46 |
| The Village School | 47 |
| Farming in Riseley | 77 |
|     High Barn Farm | 83 |
|     Harings Farm | 88 |
|     Lodge Farm | 91 |
|     Sackville Lodge Farm | 95 |
|     Sackville Nursery | 99 |
|     Mill Farm Nursery | 100 |
|     Grange Farm | 103 |
|     Red House Farm | 106 |
|     Riseley Lodge Farm | 109 |
|     Coldham Lodge Farm | 113 |
|     Town Farm | 114 |
|     Tidbury and Lowsdown Farms | 119 |
|     Lord's Farm | 120 |

|  |  |
|---|---|
| Parkers Farm | 121 |
| Dainty Farm | 121 |
| Hillview Farm | 122 |
| High Barn House | 123 |
| College Farm | 127 |
| 109 High Street | 128 |
| 71 High Street | 129 |
| 15 Gold Street | 130 |
| Shackles Field | 130 |
| Did you know that . . . | 132 |
| Earning a Living | 133 |
| The Windmills | 133 |
| Building Trades | 135 |
| Tradesmen | 138 |
| Shops in Riseley | 141 |
| Shoe Trades | 142 |
| Butchers | 144 |
| Bakers | 144 |
| Barbers | 145 |
| Blacksmiths, Garages and Agricultural Engineers | 145 |
| Carpenters and Wheelwrights | 147 |
| Lace Making | 148 |
| The Royal Aircraft Establishment | 151 |
| The Chapel Gallery | 152 |
| Brook House | 153 |
| Instrument Engineering | 155 |
| In Times of War | 157 |
| Muster Lists | 158 |
| National Defence Volunteers | 159 |
| World War One | 162 |
| World War Two | 166 |
| Evacuees | 167 |
| 'We Shall Defend Our Island' | 168 |
| 'Eyes and Ears' | 169 |
| Village at War | 170 |
| POWs | 172 |
| Over Here | 173 |
| Victory | 179 |

| | |
|---|---|
| Hostelries and Public Houses | 181 |
| Did you know that . . . | 188 |
| Famous Faces | 189 |
| Sport, Parades and Village Events | 193 |
|     Football | 193 |
|     Cricket | 195 |
|     Point to Point | 196 |
|     Bowls | 200 |
|     Badminton | 202 |
|     The Intervillage Sports Competition | 203 |
|     Walter Howard | 205 |
|     Feast Sunday | 205 |
|     The Moravian Annual Party | 206 |
|     The Annual Children's Party | 206 |
|     Coronation of George V, 1911 | 207 |
|     Coronation of Queen Elizabeth II, 1953 | 208 |
|     The Friendly Societies | 209 |
|     The Annual Fair | 212 |
|     The Floods | 214 |
| Our Village | 217 |
|     The Village Hall | 217 |
|     The Playing Field | 219 |
|     The Newsletter | 221 |
|     Policing in Riseley | 221 |
|     Parish Council | 224 |
|     Margaret Beaufort Middle School | 225 |
|     Scouting and Guiding | 228 |
|     Playgroups | 231 |
|     Mothers' Union | 233 |
|     The WEA | 234 |
|     The Women's Institute | 234 |
|     Riseley Dramatic Society and the Riseley Players | 235 |
|     Ross Meadow | 239 |
| Afterword | 241 |
| The Contributors | 243 |
| Bibliography | 247 |
| Sponsors | 248 |

## Illustrations

| | Page |
|---|---|
| Map of Riseley | xiv |
| The Pertesoil Manor – moated site | 6 |
| All Saints Church, Riseley | 11 |
| Diagrams of church construction | 12 |
| The chancel on the south side of the church | 21 |
| The chancel on the north side of the church | 24 |
| Reverend Paulson | 25 |
| Reverend Davis | 27 |
| Reverend Philips | 27 |
| Reverend Bourne | 28 |
| The chancel with dais and table | 30 |
| All Saints Church Riseley in the year 2000 | 31 |
| The famous stone on which Katharine of Aragon rested in 1534 | 32 |
| Moravian Chapel and congregation | 33 |
| Chapel Gallery, former Moravian Chapel, summer 2000 | 36 |
| The old Methodist Chapel – 1989 | 37 |
| The old Methodist Chapel | 41 |
| The new Methodist Chapel | 41 |
| The Baptist Chapel | 42 |
| The green where the Baptist Chapel used to stand | 44 |
| The School as shown on the original architect's plan | 48 |
| The School as shown in the original architect's drawings | 49 |
| A page from an 'Object Lesson' of 1897 | 58 |
| One of the earliest woodwork classes | 60 |
| School photograph – 1890 | 63 |
| Miss Waldock's Class – 1926-27 | 64 |
| Miss Waldock's Class – 1950-51 | 65 |
| Enclosure map | 78 |
| Map of parish of Riseley showing the farms | 82 |
| High Barn Farm | 83 |
| Ralph Savage with his binder | 84 |
| Engine and timber dolly | 85 |
| Engine and threshing drum, circa 1905 | 86 |
| Hoeing brussels – Lily Felce at Riseley Lodge Farm | 89 |
| Crawler tractor at Grange Farm | 90 |
| Stock yard at Lodge Farm | 91 |
| Massey-Harris bagger-combiner at Lodge Farm | 94 |
| Rickyard with thatched ricks | 96 |

| | |
|---|---|
| Charles Gardner's dispersal sale at Sackville | 97 |
| Jack Wilkinson working on the cabbage planter | 98 |
| Les Vincent in the cucumber house | 102 |
| Grange Farm House | 104 |
| Pea viner at Grange Farm | 106 |
| Muck heaps waiting to be spread | 108 |
| Riseley Lodge Farm | 110 |
| Turning hay by hand | 111 |
| Carting hay | 112 |
| Coldham Lodge Farm | 113 |
| Town Farm House | 114 |
| The clover stack – Town Farm | 116 |
| Stubble burning – Martin Harris at Grange Farm | 118 |
| Hand shearing with stack behind | 120 |
| High Barn House | 124 |
| Mowing gang, circa 1900 | 125 |
| Horse drawn binder | 126 |
| Combine harvesters at Grange Farm | 127 |
| College Farm House from the High Street | 128 |
| Threshing straw for the thatch at High Barn House, 1971 | 131 |
| The Keysoe Road windmill | 133 |
| Diagram of the layout of the brickyard and tile yard | 135 |
| 109 High Street in typical Riseley brick | 136 |
| Oscar Croot in front of Lodge Farm | 138 |
| A very early photograph of woodsmen | 138 |
| A High Street scene showing Rickett's Shop | 142 |
| Riseley Co-op | 143 |
| The Riseley Reading Rooms | 144 |
| Bob Pentlow and horses waiting to be shod | 146 |
| Ted Pentlow on his motorcycle in front of the petrol pumps | 147 |
| Eli Litchfield with a wheel he had made | 148 |
| Riseley lace school, circa 1910 | 149 |
| Betsy Fairey with her lace cushion and candle | 150 |
| Brook House in 1986 | 153 |
| Brook House restored and extended, October 1999 | 155 |
| Instrument Engineering | 156 |
| Archers at the butts | 157 |
| Riseley Muster List – 1539 | 158 |
| National Defence List for Riseley | 159 |

| | |
|---|---|
| A Bedfordshire Militia Man – 1803 | 160 |
| Wilfred Ashworth | 162 |
| 'Clary' Bateman | 162 |
| Aubrey Savage | 163 |
| John George Rootham | 163 |
| Land girl Carolyn (Carrie) Partridge at Town Farm | 164 |
| 'Tink' Hancock and Donkey Cart | 164 |
| Armistice Day, Riseley | 165 |
| Children celebrating the Armistice on Gold Street bridge | 165 |
| 'Steve' Stevens and Leslie Hawkins | 166 |
| Royal Observer Corps Post, Riseley | 169 |
| Lily Felce | 171 |
| Mary Wallis | 171 |
| B-17 'Eager Beaver' and personnel | 174 |
| Bomb stack in Pippin Wood | 174 |
| B-17s returning after their 200th mission | 176 |
| The crashed B-17 in the old brickyard | 177 |
| American Servicemen in Riseley Church | 178 |
| ROC Post 1967 | 179 |
| The White Horse | 182 |
| The Five Bells | 183 |
| The Boot | 184 |
| The Red Lion | 184 |
| The Fox and Hounds, circa 1910 | 185 |
| The Swan | 186 |
| The Royal Oak, with sheep in the street | 186 |
| The George and Dragon, now 2 Waldocks Close | 187 |
| 135 High Street | 188 |
| The Prince of Wales at the Point to Point | 191 |
| Book covers featuring Riseley people and places | 192 |
| Riseley Football Club, 1920-21 | 194 |
| 1986-87 Division 5 Champions | 194 |
| Riseley Cricket team, circa 1950 | 196 |
| Procession of cars leaving the Point to Point | 197 |
| A Programme for the Point to Point | 198 |
| The start and finish of the Point to Point | 199 |
| A juggler performing at the Point to Point | 199 |
| The bowling green at The White Horse | 200 |
| Players at the bowling green | 201 |

| | |
|---|---|
| Annual presentation evening for the indoor Bowls Club | 202 |
| Shotley Sports 1983 | 204 |
| Riseley Feast Parade | 205 |
| The Moravian Party, circa 1920 | 206 |
| Annual Children's Party, circa 1960 | 207 |
| Villagers celebrate the coronation | 207 |
| Procession to celebrate King George's coronation | 208 |
| A ship float just passing 93 High Street | 208 |
| A tractor towed float outside 78 High Street | 209 |
| The Foresters outside The Royal Oak | 210 |
| The parade forming up at the junction of Keysoe Road | 210 |
| The parade in later years processing past The Fox and Hounds | 211 |
| The parade in Gold Street | 211 |
| Children at the annual fair | 212 |
| Soldiers in uniform enjoying the fair, circa 1914 | 212 |
| Merry go round outside The Five Bells | 213 |
| Maypole dancing, around 1935 | 213 |
| 'Hooking the bottles', circa 1935 | 214 |
| Harry Brown climbing the greasy pole around 1925 | 214 |
| Russ Warren, the butcher, negotiating the flood | 215 |
| Floods in 1992 | 215 |
| An early picture of flooding at Gold Street bridge | 216 |
| Jock Wesley riding his horse through a flood in about 1960 | 216 |
| Old Village Hall | 217 |
| Programme for opening of village hall | 218 |
| The New Village Hall | 219 |
| Souvenir programme for the opening of Riseley Playing Field | 220 |
| Sergeant Crowsley outside Cherry Trees, 76 High Street | 222 |
| The police house – 131 High Street | 223 |
| The new police post | 223 |
| Margaret Beaufort School | 227 |
| Riseley Scout Band outside Daintry House | 228 |
| Queen's Guides, 10 October 1993 | 231 |
| The playgroup Nativity play, Christmas 1992 | 232 |
| The Mothers' Union | 234 |
| The Women's Institute visit to the Wedgewood Factory – 1959 | 235 |
| Drama in the old village hall | 236 |
| Riseley Dramatic Society, summer 2000 | 238 |
| Ross Meadow | 240 |

## Good Faith

This book has been created, compiled and published by the people of Riseley, both past and present.

In the process of research and collation of material, every reasonable effort has been made to ensure that it is accurate and factual. Whilst acknowledging the invaluable contribution made by those whose distant memories have been recorded here, it is recognised that such memories have been provided and repeated in good faith.

Neither the publishers, the contributors or the owners of any material contained in this book accept any liability for any errors, mistakes, misrepresentations or inaccuracies which may inadvertently have been included.

# Riseley Historical Society
## Mike Ives

Riseley Historical Society came into being during a pleasant chat over a pint of beer in the Village Hall. One evening in August 1998, I was asked what the village was doing to celebrate the Millennium. My reply was, *'nothing in particular that I am aware of, but it would be nice if we could produce a book on the history of Riseley'*.

Having lived in the village for some 30 years, I could think of many people who would be interested in this project. I contacted some of these people and our first meeting was held on 17 August 1998. Attendees were Andrew Gell, Jon Handforth, Mike Ives, Colin and Barbara Jones, Phillip Nicholls, Peter Smith and Florence Wilkinson. The meeting agreed that there was a great need for existing historical information to be gathered and for facts about the village to be recorded before they were lost. A formal committee was set up – the Riseley Millennium Book Committee was formed!

When the committee realised that the project was sufficiently important and of such a scale, a formal constitution was drawn up and charitable status applied for – the Riseley Historical Society was born. The committee was enlarged to include Julia Jarman, Sue Davies and William Wallis. Mary Shiers and Marjorie Bosman agreed to help with the word processing of the book.

The momentous task of gathering material began. The assistance of the County Records Office was sought. Kevin Ward (County Archivist) came to the next meeting and provided invaluable advice on the use of the Records Office. Many interviews were conducted with local residents to record an oral history of the village.

This book, "Riseley – Our Village", is our first publication. It has been totally generated from within the village and would not have been possible without the generosity of village residents and organisations together with the enthusiasm and commitment of all involved.

Riseley – Our Village

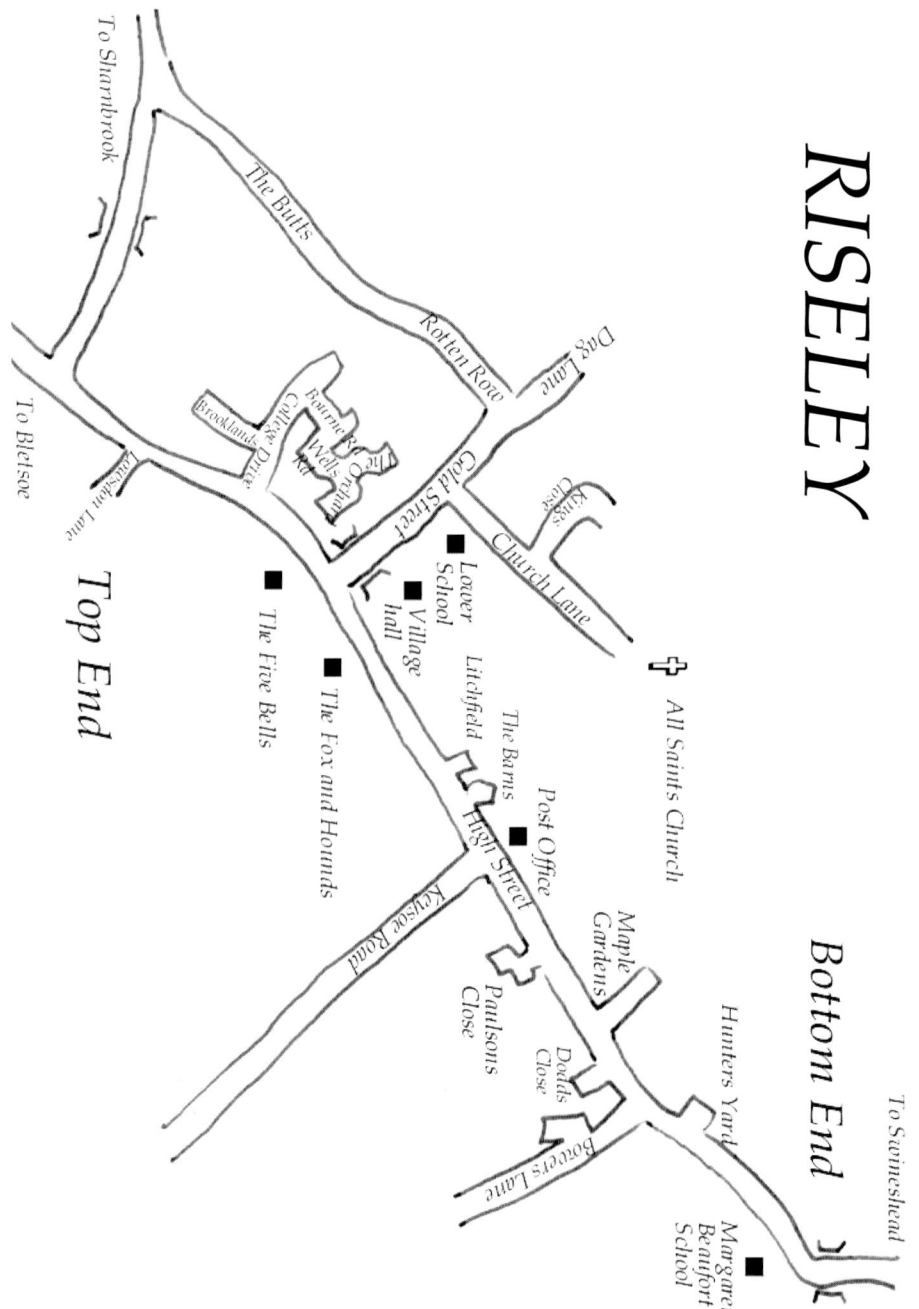

# Foreword
## John Ashworth

"Riseley – Our Village" captures the time when a self-sufficient and stable village society and the agricultural economy, which supported it, disappeared. Until the 1960s Riseley seemed very isolated to boys like me, from Luton, and my London cousins. Our uncle's farm, Park Farm, between Riseley and Bletsoe and now an art studio, had no electricity, no mains water and no mains sewage. A lifestyle survived there that had more in common with the 18th than the latter part of the 20th century. We loved it and spent as much time there as our parents and the bus timetables would allow. My Uncle, Jack Ingle had a mixed farm with horses, cattle and pigs as well as meadows and arable fields. The farm buildings and animals; Galsey wood; the 'drome and the fields and ponds around provided us boys with an adventure playground that few children enjoy today. We could be useful too, and at harvest time we felt very adult when there were cart horses to be led, sheaves to be put into stooks (dirty, backbreaking work I remember) and rabbits to be caught as the binder cut the last of the corn (much more fun).

Until rationing went in the early 1950s, the farm provided the most delicious things we ate. During the war my Aunt Nancy's homemade bread, butter, sausages and ham were simply lifesavers. There was very little else that she wanted and most of that could be bought in Riseley. Occasional trips to the Co-op with side visits to Granddad Ashworth in the High Street for bullseyes feature prominently in my memories of the 1940s. Virtually everything that broke on the farm could be repaired – either by Mr Pentlow, the blacksmith, or Mr Litchfield, the carpenter. Trips to get the horses reshod were the best because I was allowed to ride them on the way back. Of course, life was hard for the grown-ups. My Uncle always seemed tired and after the German POWs went back, there were never enough farmworkers to help him do all the things, like the ditching and hedging, that he thought should be done. A farmer's wife also had a hard life without electric appliances to help with the cooking and housework and the dogs, cats and hens not to mention us children and the farm accounts to be looked after. I am amazed that Aunt Nancy put up with us all, but she did and very cheerfully too as I remember.

However, in the 1950s the resumption of trade in agricultural products and the widespread availability of tractors and combine harvesters undermined the profitability of small mixed farms like Park Farm. Change was inevitable and with the disappearance of the horses, pigs and cattle came the appearance of mains electricity and TV, mains water and sewage and above all motor cars and easy mobility. Riseley's isolation was coming to an end as new houses brought new people who could work more than a couple of miles away from Gold Street.

But communities are more than houses and it is important that memories are preserved. "Riseley – Our Village" has caught, in the words and memories of the Gells and the Litchfields, the Felces and the Sharmans, what it was like to live through the most profound change in British rural life since the Enclosure Act in the 18th century. The old order survived in North Bedfordshire longer than elsewhere, I suspect, and so change, when it did come, was all the more rapid. This book provides a fascinating and very particular account of what that meant for one village. I cannot think of a more appropriate way of celebrating the start of a new millennium than to preserve the memories of those who lived through those times and provided the foundations of the present thriving community.

John Ashworth<br>
Chairman of the Board of the British Library<br>
August 2000

# A Clearing in the Brushwood
Andrew Gell

Two thousand years ago the part of Bedfordshire now occupied by the Parish of Riseley was largely a wooded area, with just a few peasant families living in crude timber and mud dwellings roofed with thatch. They eked a living from the woodlands, hunting the wild animals that roamed there, keeping swine that were left to forage in the woods and cultivating a few basic crops in clearings. The brook would have been an important feature in early Riseley as a source of water for drinking and for watering the crops. Set in a valley as Riseley is now, it would have been a sheltered place to live.

To find the first written mention of the settlement linked to the modern day village we have to by-pass 800 years of the first millennium – the years of Roman occupation and the Dark Ages that followed – till we reach the beginning of the 9th century.

At that time the countryside was enjoying a period of peace and tranquillity. The settlement was part of the Kingdom of Mercia that covered most of Central England and it is in this Saxon period that the name of the settlement is first recorded. Three different spellings can be found - RISA'S LEAH, HRIS LEAH and RISLAI. The translation means *'a clearing in the brushwood'*, echoing the very rural nature of the village.

In the Domesday Book of 1086, the version used was RISLAI and over the next few hundred years this evolved into the modern spelling that we use today. The local population would have been made up of a mixture of native races and some Ancient Britons, Anglo Saxons and probably some of Roman descent.

At the end of the first millennium the area of Central England became sub-divided into areas known as the Midland Shires; hence Northamptonshire, Bedfordshire, Cambridgeshire. These were further sub-divided into measurements of land known as hides. Bedfordshire is recorded as consisting of 1200 hides. These were not accurately measured areas of land but a hide was roughly described as, *'land sufficient for cultivation by one plough in a year or to support one household'*.

Depending on the nature of the land the hides varied in size. Roughly this could be between 60 and 120 modern day acres. The number of hides was significant because it was used to determine the number of soldiers that could be called upon to serve the King in time of war.

The shires were further divided up, for ease of administration, into areas known as Hundreds. Bedfordshire had nine full Hundreds and three half Hundreds. The north of the county was called the Stodden Hundred and consisted of the present day villages of Riseley, Knotting, Yielden, Dean and Shelton, Melchbourne, Keysoe, Bolnhurst, Pertenhall, Little Staughton and Tilbrook. Note that Swineshead was not included, as it was part of Huntingdonshire at this time.

A gathering known as the Stodden Court would meet every four weeks to discuss local matters and concerns, and deal with matters of law. The King's representative, the Sheriff (originally Shire's Reeve), presided over these Stodden Courts. The Courts were held in the open air and the Court for the Stodden Hundred is recorded as being held in a field at Pertenhall. Unfortunately, no records exist of what was discussed at these meetings.

This period of peace came to an end during the 9th and 10th centuries with the invasion of the Danes. It is known that they came up the River Ouse and had settlements at Sharnbrook, Carlton and Renhold. It is almost certain, therefore, that they came to Riseley.

The boundary between the part of England in the control of King Alfred and the Danelaw, which was the part of the country controlled by the Danes, ran along the Roman Watling Street, now the A5. There were constant skirmishes along the boundary. For the villagers of Riseley these must have been uncertain times. After intense fighting between 917 and 924 the land was regained from the Danes by King Edward The Elder, son of Alfred. The Danes regained this area by 1042 under the rule of King Canute. It is rumoured that some of the timber-framed houses in Riseley contain timbers salvaged from abandoned Danish longboats.

It is in this period leading up to the Battle of Hastings in 1066 and the Norman invasion of England that we find the first definite details of who lived in the village. The Domesday Book records who owned the land in Riseley prior to the Norman Conquest:

**The Sheriff, Godric** who was a thane of King Edward (thane was a representative of the King, in rank between that of a hereditary nobleman and a freeman) held 2$^1$/$_2$ hides of land – between 150-300 acres. He actually owned the land as it was recorded that, *'he could do what he would with it'*.
**Burgred** held 2 hides in Lordship from the King and six of his men shared a further 4 hides of land, which they owned and could do with as they wanted. Quite a substantial holding which was recorded as being worth 100 shillings (£5). One of these men was called Alwin and he also held land in Newton Bromswold but this was owned by Burgred and he could not grant it to anyone else or sell it without Burgred's permission. The other five men are not known.
**Honday**, Earl Harold's man held 1 hide from the King but he could sell it or do with it what he would. It was valued at 10 shillings (50p).
**Alwin**, not Burgred's Alwin, but a different Alwin, who was Lord of the Manor of Elvedon, held $^1$/$_2$ hide valued at 5 shillings (25p).
**Askell**, who was another thane of King Edward and held the manors of Bletsoe and Putnoe, held 1 hide of land. He was clearly an important man as he also held Keysoe and a manor at Colmworth.

Then came the invasion of England by William the Conqueror in 1066, the death of King Harold and the beginning of Norman rule. In Riseley, as in most of England, land was taken from its previous owners and given to Normans and supporters of William.

Most of the thanes of King Edward and King Harold either fled or were killed in the fighting. It is known that Godric, who had held 2$^1$/$_2$ hides of land in Riseley, was killed at the Battle of Hastings. The change to Norman rule was a big change for the villagers of Riseley. The landowners who they had known for many years were swept away and replaced by strangers.

The Domesday Book, completed in 1086 during the reign of William the Conqueror to record the assets and population of his new Kingdom, was a medieval form of census. It tells us how many heads of family there were and who in Riseley was given land after the conquest.

Godric, killed at the Battle of Hastings, had his land divided between the Bishop Remigius of Lincoln, who passed it to his man Godfrey, Alric the Priest and Osbern, son of Richard. This land had one plough and supported one villager, five smallholders and 20 pigs.

Burgred also lost his land to the Bishop of Lincoln who passed it to be held by two Frenchmen and six Englishmen. This was a large holding and had seven ploughs with six villagers, seven smallholders and one slave to work the land. It supported 20 pigs.

Honday lost his hide to King William to be held by David of Argenton. It had one plough, one villager and three smallholders. No pigs are recorded.

Alwin's 1/2 hide went to Osbern, son of Richard, and was held by Hugh Hubold. It had only one smallholder and was half cultivated and half meadow.

Askell lost his land to Hugh of Beauchamp. It had two ploughs, but no villagers or smallholders are recorded. It is listed as an outlier of Keysoe which Hugh also held and it is assumed that it was worked by nine villagers, six smallholders and one slave which he had at Keysoe with five ploughs.

From these details we can estimate the population of Riseley in 1086. Unfortunately, only the heads of houses were recorded and not the complete families. The number taken from the Domesday survey for Riseley totalled 24 – eight villagers and 16 smallholders. If we assume each would have had a wife and say an average of four children then we have a total population in the region of 100 to 150 people. We can only guess at the exact figure.

Life in Riseley after the Conquest continued to be very rural with agriculture the only industry. Life revolved around the seasons and was hard. It is thought that the village at this time was centred on the area where the church now stands. The only dwellings would have been crudely built of timber and mud construction with thatched roofs. All signs of their existence, if this theory is correct, have long since disappeared.

During the period after the Norman Conquest we find very few references to Riseley in historical records. The official language in England at this time was Latin and the village must have felt very isolated.

The Normans introduced the manorial system of control and this was firmly established by 1200.

The average size of a manorial holding in North Bedfordshire is recorded as 390 acres whereas the average size throughout Bedfordshire was 600 acres for multi-manor parishes and 1200 acres for single manor parishes.

The Lord of the Manor was responsible for looking after the land under his control and the peasants working that land. He was a powerful person, responsible to the King for law and order and collection of taxes. In Riseley three manors are recorded and the signs of two of them still remain – the moated sites of the Lawrence's at Lodge Farm and the Pertesoil's in the fields behind Hunters Yard.

**The Pertesoil Manor** site is extensive, with not only the moated site where the manor stood but also the sites of the fishponds used for supplying fresh fish to the house and the circular dovecote for fresh meat. This is the earliest manor site recorded. There is a record in 1202-03 of William, son of Azon, quitclaiming (giving up) 65 acres of land to William Pertesoil and Robert Rufus, this land enfeoffed (handed over from) Simon de Beauchamp to be held by knights service.

In 1234 there was a shortage of knights in the country and in an effort to increase the number the King directed his Sheriffs to list all men of a certain standing who had £15 worth of land in Bedfordshire. One of these men listed was Simon Pertesoil of Riseley. It is not recorded whether Simon became a knight but it is noted that being a knight meant being called up for war services. As these were times of foreign wars it was not unknown for the Sheriff to be bribed to avoid being called to be a knight!

Simon Pertesoil is also mentioned in 1240 when jurors were being sought for the County Courts. The jury system was just beginning and there was a shortage of educated men to serve at the County Court. Such men from the *'Hundreds'* were sought and from the Stodden Hundred Simon was selected. Simon is listed as being a Lord of the Manor in 1288 and if this is the same Simon as mentioned in 1234 he was Lord for at least 54 years which was a very long period bearing in mind the early mortality of the time.

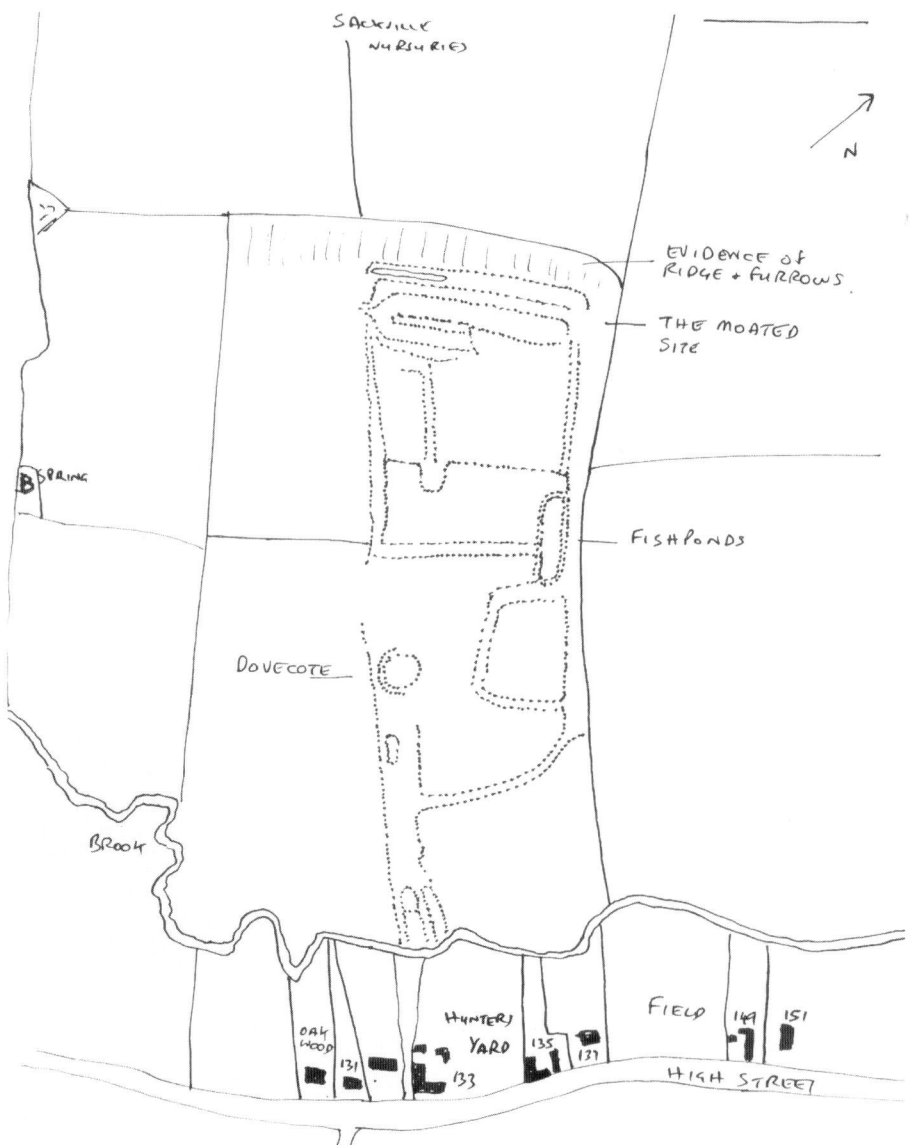

*The Pertesoil Manor – moated site*

Simon held some land at Pertenhall for which he paid two shillings (10p) annually to his overlord William de Monchesney. He also leased a dwelling and outbuildings plus 2 hides of land in Riseley to a Philip Burnell in 1278 for eight years. Philip died in 1282 and the land reverted to Simon. John Pertesoil succeeded his father Simon and is recorded as Lord in 1302 and by his son Roger Pertesoil in 1316.

Thirty years later in 1346 William Pertesoil met with a violent end in the parish, being *'murdered of set design and purpose'*. John Pertesoil became Lord of the Manor.

The manor continued in the Pertesoil family until 1439 when another William Pertesoil died and there was an attempt by his two sisters, Elizabeth Rous and Athelina Sackville to claim the property. Thomas Sackville, son of Athelina, owned other land in Riseley adjacent to Pertesoil land where Sackville Farm now stands. The sisters were unsuccessful and the manor went to John Pertesoil who was the illegitimate son of William. The last record of a Pertesoil as Lord of the Manor is in 1518 when Robert Pertesoil died and left the land to his grandson John. Reference to the Pertesoil Manor disappeared for 113 years until 1631 when it was owned by a Richard Tabbot. It was passed to Thomas Tabbot in 1631, then to Adam Hill in 1656 and then to John Hale in 1685. Reference then ceases completely.

**The Manor of Lawrence** was sited on the field adjacent to Lodge Farm and the moat is still there today. It is recorded in 1279 as being held by William Lawrence and then passed to a Robert Broughton and then to his grandson, also Robert. Robert's son, John, sold it to a Richard Fox, who was Bishop of Winchester. He passed it on to William Holgyll and then to Sir Anthony Oughtred in 1530. He passed it to his brother-in-law, Sir Edward Seymour. Edward was the brother of Jane Seymour, third wife of Henry VIII. He later became Lord Protector Somerset in the minority of his nephew Edward VI. He sold the manor to St John of Bletsoe and it was then merged with the rest of the St John estates.

**The third Manor was that of the Harveys** and the site is not known. It is believed to have been the area of Coldham Farm but this cannot be confirmed. The manor was part of the Knights' Hospitaller possessions in Riseley and Melchbourne and is recorded as such in 1279. It was held for the Knights Templar by Walter the son of Geoffrey of Riseley, passing to William son of Lawrence of Riseley and is recorded as being owned by John, another son of Geoffrey of Riseley in 1320.

John Harvey is recorded as owning the manor in 1351 and this is known as he fell victim to the Black Death, which swept England between 1350 and 1360. Such was the fear of the plague that following the death of John Harvey no one wanted to take possession of his 300 acres for 100 years. The next record is of ownership by Agnes, the wife of another descendant of John Harvey, in 1473. It went to her son, George, in 1510 when Agnes moved to Paxton near Peterborough. George Harvey sold it to Thomas Sackville who was a member of the Royal Household. He had borrowed money from the King and was unable to repay it so the manor was passed to the King for a term of years (the number is not recorded).

It was leased to Lady Radcliffe from 1555 to 1562, but in 1557 the lease was passed back to the Sackvilles. The manor then went through five more owners between 1557 and 1759 when it was sold to the Duke of Bedford and then into the St John estates when the Duke of Bedford sold his land to the St Johns of Bletsoe.

The Black Death, which was a form of bubonic plague carried by black rats and transmitted by fleas, was a disaster for small communities and Riseley did not escape. It is believed that one third of the population died. The plague was seen as a blight on the land and it can be certain that just as no one wanted to work John Harvey's land, the surviving villagers would not have wanted to remain in dwellings where the plague had been. They would have burned their homes and moved to different locations.

The main village is assumed to have moved from around the church to its present site in a linear arrangement along the brook resulting in the long narrow village, with the church separated by fields from it, that we have today.

The shape of our village was also being transformed by the transfer of ownership of land from small manorial units farmed by peasants to the ownership of large wealthy estates farmed by tenant farmers and peasant workers.

In the 1530s came the Reformation by Henry VIII. John and Oliver St John of Bletsoe were the County representatives of the Reformation Parliament and were therefore in a position of some power.

They obtained the Lordship of the Manor of Bolnhurst from Thorney Abbey and Keysoe Grange from Chicksands Priory in 1559. During this time the Lords of St John were also acquiring additional land in Riseley as can be seen from our information on the manors of Lawrence and Harvey. They became the largest landowners in our village. The title of Lord of the Manor of Riseley was until recent years held by the St John family. It was sold in the 1980s when the trend was to sell off redundant titles!

The Duke of Bedford was also a large landowner in Riseley and this also emanated from Henry VIII. As a gift in his will, Henry VIII gave the Manor of Woburn to one of his trustees, John Russell. In 1550 he was created the Earl of Bedford – the foundation of the present Duke of Bedford estates at Woburn. He acquired the preceptor at Melchbourne and its land and built up a substantial holding. The drawing up of the Enclosure Map in 1793, when all the land was enclosed, showed the St John family and the Duke of Bedford to be the main landowners.

The estate system of ownership by these wealthy families remained right through to 1951 when, like many great estates throughout England, the changes in the 20th century and the effects of two great wars changed life forever. In Riseley, parts of the St John estate were sold off as early as 1930. The remainder of the estate was finally sold off in 1952 by auction and farmers, who had previously been tenants, were able to buy their land. Larger enterprises moved in by buying up others.

Villagers who had lived in estate owned cottages were given the opportunity to buy their own cottage. Most did so and the cottages usually went for a set price. The going rate was £60 per cottage. This may seem a minute sum by today's values, but for the average manual worker it was still a substantial amount to find in the 1950s! An interesting anecdote from this period is the amusing tale of a resident buying her cottage from the estate for £60, which was less than she had just paid for one of the first black and white televisions!

The break up of the estate into private ownership of the housing stock and much of the land in the village was the beginning of modern Riseley. Up until then village life had changed very little; work was rural, agricultural and self-contained within the village. Villagers were relatively poor and were tenants rather than property owners. The estate break up changed that and with private ownership came the buying and selling of properties and new residents moving in. New house building followed, as more parcels of land became available for building. The building boom of the 1960s and 1970s shaped the village as we know it today. Many villagers now travel to larger towns and to London for their employment. A change that took some 50 years at most, replaced a millennium of life and work and self-sufficiency within the village!

### Did you know that . . .

*In May 1274, a poor child named Joan was drowned in the brook. This is one of the earliest recorded happenings in Riseley. It is said that she drowned at Fordebrigge, which we think is the part of the brook adjacent to the new Police post where the Wellbourne footbridge is now.*

# All Saints Church - The People and their Building
Phillip Nicholls

*All Saints Church, Riseley*

Riseley Church took shape, both inside and out, over several hundred years. The present building is unlikely to have been the first parish church, although it may be on or near the site of an earlier, probably timber constructed, church. A recent report by the County Archaeologist suggests that in the early 12th century there was a small nave for the people and a chancel for the altar and priest. With the exception of part of the foundation of the north wall, none of this early church building survives. In the 13th century a south aisle and chapel were built against the original nave. It is known that the chapel projected beyond the original chancel, as there is a window of this date in the north wall of the chapel. The nave was lengthened westward at the same time.

At some time in the 14th century, the length of the chancel was extended to that of the south chapel and a new interconnecting arch was built. The sides of the arch have notches and slots, marking where a screen was fitted. The extension of the chancel resulted in the removal of the original chancel arch, which was not replaced. At about this time a rood screen was built beneath a preaching loft and the main part of the tower was built. It was heightened in the 15th century. The porch is also 15th century.

*Diagrams of church construction showing the order in which it was built*

After the 15th century, the south chapel was used as a chancel and the north chancel as a chapel. This arrangement is mentioned in a document dated 1839. Sixteenth century documents note that in 1548 there was a chantry chapel. This could explain why a rectangular squint, which has been cut through the wall between the chancel and chapel, is on a diagonal axis. This would have allowed the priest at the altar in the north chantry chapel to see the priest officiating at the high altar in the south chancel.

Among the many new religious orders, which came into being in the 11th and 12th centuries, were the military-religious orders of the Knights Templar and Knights Hospitaller. These orders became known as the Order of St John of Jerusalem. It was they who were given the patronage of All Saints by Alice de Clermont in 1224. They kept the patronage until the Dissolution, when in 1539 the crown took it over. In 1585-86 Queen Elizabeth granted the patronage to Sir Christopher Hatton. By 1618 it had become the property of Oliver St John of Bletsoe and remained with that family until 1957 when it was taken over by The Martyrs' Memorial and Church of England Trust, who administer the patronage of some 500 parishes. The patron has the right to nominate a clergyman to a living, although the diocesan bishop has the right to reject the nominee. The patron was also responsible for the upkeep of the chancel.

It is interesting to note that in 1291 the value of the church was put at £4 5s 8d (£4.28), and at the Dissolution had gained in value to £8 17s 10d (£8.89).

Riseley was originally in the diocese of Dorchester but by 1086, when the Domesday Book was written, came within the diocese of Lincoln. The Bishop of Lincoln had land in Riseley at that time as did the Norman bishop, Godfrey, Bishop of Coutance. From the Domesday Book we also learn that the priest at the time was Alric, and he shared a holding belonging to Hugh de Beauchamp.

There are lists of clergy on either side of the vestry door in the church, the first name on it being the rector Fulco de Monte Acuto. The clergy named after him are all vicars as a vicarage, in place of the rectory, was constituted in 1249. The distinction being, for a rector all the tithes were attached to the benefice for the maintenance of the incumbent. When the Knights were given the patronage, they appear to have taken over the tithes and appointed a vicar to administer the church. It is important to remember that until the Reformation the church was Catholic. The services would have been held in Latin, so unless they were well educated, the members of the congregation would not have understood anything the priest was saying.

Little is known about the clergy of All Saints until John Harding MA, who served from 1690 until his death in 1742 at the age of 87. It was he who began to enter the fatal ailments of his parishioners throughout that time. They are entered in the oldest surviving register dating from 1626. It is the outstanding feature of the register and certainly the most uncommon.

| | | | | | |
|---|---|---|---|---|---|
| Fever | 168 | Infants | 144 | Consumption | 62 |
| Old Age | 38 | Dropsy | 30 | Smallpox | 27 |
| Complications | 23 | Childbed | 15 | Suddenly | 14 |
| | | | | | |
| Ague | 1 | Grief | 1 | Scrofula | 1 |
| Apoplexy | 4 | Hurt with a stick | 1 | Scurvy | 3 |
| Asthma | 5 | Ilium passio (Pain of the Groin) | 1 | Sore leg | 2 |
| Bled to death | 1 | Jaundice, black | 1 | Spitting of blood | 1 |
| Burned to death | 1 | Killed by a cart | 3 | Spleen | 1 |
| Cancer | 4 | Killed by a horse | 1 | Spotted fever | 1 |
| Chin cough | 8 | Lethargy | 2 | Stagnation of blood | 1 |
| Cholic | 8 | Lice, eaten up of | 4 | Starved | 6 |
| Convulsions | 8 | Long illness | 8 | Surfoit | 3 |
| Diabetes | 2 | Looseness | 4 | Tymphany | 1 |
| Diarrhoea | 1 | No one knows | 1 | Ulcer | 1 |
| Discontent | 1 | Overlaid infant | 2 | Urine, bloody | 1 |
| Drinking fever by | 1 | Palsy | 2 | Urine, stoppage of | 1 |
| Drowned | 8 | Pleurisy | 5 | Vomiting | 1 |
| Fever upon the spirits | 1 | Quinsy | 4 | Want of looking to | 2 |
| Fits, sounding | 1 | Rotten | 1 | Water in the head | 1 |
| Fistula | 1 | Rupture | 1 | Worms | 4 |
| Flux, bloody | 1 | Scalded | 1 | Unspecified | 45 |
| Gangrene | 2 | Scarlet Fever | 2 | | |

These illnesses give a sorry picture of economic conditions in Riseley. It is sad to read how high infant mortality was, as well as the number who died from fever and consumption. Of the 701 recorded deaths only 38 are attributed to old age.

**The Church Vestry**
The oldest surviving registers are kept at the County Records Office in Bedford, and contain interesting information about the church and the wide authority it had over village affairs. There was no parish council until the end of the 19th century and of course no health service, family income support or child benefit. To deal with these matters and the upkeep of the village, the church held an annual *'Easter vestry meeting of Parishioners'*. At this meeting two churchwardens were elected - the vicar's warden, whose staff of office is topped with a mitre, and the people's warden, whose staff is topped with a crown. The present staffs are at the end of two pews in the church. They were presented to the church in memory of John Lowe, who for many years was organist, choirmaster and Sunday School teacher, by his widow in 1938. Also, each year a guardian of the poor and an overseer of the poor were elected together with two surveyors of the bye ways.

The vicar chaired the meetings during the year which were usually held in the vestry of the church, but sometimes at The Boot Inn opposite Gold Street bridge. A rate was fixed for the relief of the poor in the village, in 1855 a rate of 1s (5p) in the pound was collected. In addition to that, in 1858 some houses were rated between £1 5s 0d (£1.25) and £2 0s 0d. At the annual meeting in 1859, having elected the officers, the meeting agreed that land belonging to the parish should be sold for 1s 6d (7$^{1}$/2p) a rood (a quarter of an acre). Later that year it was agreed to rebuild the parish pound, which was used to confine stray animals, near the turnpike road (now the entrance to Sharnbrook road). Sometimes church business was discussed - in 1862 it was noted that costs of divine services were estimated by the churchwardens to be £12 10s 0d (£12.50), and for repairs £11 0s 0d. For these purposes, a church rate of 2d (less than 1p) in the pound was proposed and granted. A church rate continued until 1946 by which time each collector had a small book to note who paid and how much they paid.

In 1866 there was an outbreak of cholera in London and elsewhere. A meeting was held where it was suggested by Revd R N Durrant (curate) that the purchase of four gallons of Condy's disinfectant fluid should be made for distribution throughout the parish, as a precautionary step against the disease. Revd Durrant and Mr Banks volunteered to go round the parish to distribute it, with the assistance of a man to carry the pail. Mr Banks would offer simple medical advice to prevent the disease and guidance in case of an attack of diarrhoea or of the disease itself.

Human disease was not the only problem. On Easter Monday 1867, it was agreed that a sum of about £5 collected during an outbreak of cattle disease (foot and mouth?) should be retained for another year to meet any emergency that might still arise. This cattle plague added further problems. The cattle used to go into the churchyard and feed on grass and because of the disease could no longer do so. It was agreed to ask the vicar to contribute the herbage of the churchyard; in return the parishioners generally would undertake to level the churchyard where needed and keep in good condition, graves, paths, gates and fences. It was recommended that the grass be mowed four times a year.

In 1871 another duty fell upon the church vestry. To meet the requirements of the Government Board of Education, application was made for funds to furnish the National School with forms, desks and other things necessary. A voluntary rate of 1$^1$/2d (less than 1p) in the pound was agreed to meet these requirements. A committee was set up to provide these for the school. On the 30 May the new vicar Revd J J Blick took the chair, the Hon Andrew St John was present as were 14 parishioners (there were usually only four or five). At this meeting the first committee of management was formed to carry out the business of the school. The following were elected:- Revd J J Blick, vicar, Revd M Cooke, Moravian minister, Mr Samuel Francis, Mr Banks and Mr Bolton – the trustees of the school ex officio.

Later that year discussions were held with respect to enlarging the school to provide accommodation for the number of children according to government requirements. Daniel Rootham's contract was accepted and in addition he was to build earth closets of the same plan as those at Souldrop school. Building work was to start in the spring of 1873.

It should be remembered that the parishes financed themselves – there was no education authority as we have today. The parishes raised their own rates, and so an offer was made by Lord St John towards the cost of Daniel Rootham's contract until a rate for the enlargement of the school was collected. Four parishioners were asked to contribute £6 each for the same purpose. Whilst this work was going on, the schoolmaster's house was to be papered and painted and the boys' school painted. The headmaster was to pay a rent of 5s (25p) a year.

No further mention is made of the school until May 1888, when the vestry requested Lord St John to convey to the parish the piece of land upon which the school was built. Lord St John replied that, as tenant for life, he had no power to comply with their request. However, he proposed that two representatives, Mr Bower and Mr Graham, should go and see the Revd Young, late vicar of Riseley and surviving trustee, to suggest that he appoint three trustees for the school. This was done and Lord St John, Revd Henry L Graham, vicar, and Mr Bower were appointed trustees of the portion of the school buildings. A voluntary school rate of 3d (about $1^1/_2$p) in the pound was to be collected.

The school expenses were met in various ways. In April 1885 it was agreed that the grass from the sides of the road should be let in various lots for a year. The churchwardens would oversee this and the way warden would be empowered to carry out this proposal. The money raised would go towards school expenses.

At the November meeting 1873, it was reported that Samuel Richards had died and left £200. One hundred pounds was bequeathed to the parish of Riseley, the interest arising from it to be applied to the support of the Sunday School of the established church for ever. The other £100 and the interest from it was to be given *'to the necessitous industrious poor in bread, who frequent the established church, on St Thomas day for ever'*. The trustees appointed were the vicar and churchwardens, and this remains so. On St Thomas' Day in 1885 nearly 500 loaves were made. The charity now pays £2.28 per annum to the Sunday School and an equal amount to the vicar's discretionary fund.

There are three other charities. Two, Cakebread Close and Bourne's Gift have now been combined. Cakebread Close Charity was originally vested solely in the vicar of the parish by virtue of a piece of land being given to him at the time of the Enclosure Act in the 18th century. It was given on the basis that he should take *'two bushels of wheat'* being part of the annual proceeds of that land and make it *'into equal cakes and bread, and distribute alike, to every householder in the parish, on Good Friday, for ever'*. There is now a new condition to the charity as a result of the land, approximately half an acre, being sold in 1977 as the site of the new vicarage. The Charity still allows Hot Cross Buns (Cakebread) to be distributed to those attending the service on Good Friday, but the greater proportion of the income, resulting from the sale of the land and the investment of the capital, is now administered by the trustees who are the vicar, a nominee of the Parochial Church Council and a nominee of the Parish Council.

Bourne's Gift was given and invested at the time of the Napoleonic Wars for the benefit of widows in the parish. It was in the first instance only £10, but now that it has been combined with the Cakebread Close Charity, the interest provides enough money for each widow to receive £3.01 at Christmas. In recent years widowers have also been included.

The third charity is Corn Close, the field between the new vicarage and the church. The rent from this two acre field goes towards the maintenance of the church building.

It was at their August meeting in 1884 that the vestry meeting had to deal with what might be considered an unsavoury matter. The brook needed cleaning out. A large portion of it belonged to the Highways Board but the rest to small occupiers, the brook also being the main sewer. For the benefit of the villagers, the Highways Board was asked to undertake the work. However, it was agreed that the material taken out should remain the property of the parish. In 1890 the Bedford Rural Sanitary Authority asked the vestry to consider the state of the brook. It was agreed that the Highways Board should be responsible for the condition of the brook.

From this time onwards various other committees of the council were notified if work needed doing in the parish. For example, in July 1891 the Highways Committee of the Council in Bedford was asked to raise the level of the High Street as it was thought that the reason it kept flooding was because it was so low.  They were also asked to improve the bottom of the new bridge at the north end of the parish near the lodge, as the original design obstructed the flow of water.  Lord St John was asked to bring these matters before the County Council at the earliest opportunity.

The powers of running the parish were gradually taken away from the church, then at the March meeting in 1894 the crunch came and the following motion was passed.  *'This meeting desires to express regret at the end of the old order of Parish Government, and while willing loyally to carry out this new regime considers that change was uncalled for, is likely to prove more expensive, and certifies to the peaceful and cordial manner in which affairs have been conducted under the old system for so many generations.'*

At the Easter vestry meeting in April 1895 the vicar, on taking the chair, remarked that, *'under the new Local Government Act (1894) matters concerning water and rates would be in the hands of the Parish Council, thus leaving the church people and wardens in a better position as regards their own affairs'*.  There had obviously been some reluctance to this change as he also asked that all would rise to the occasion and no longer pursue a policy of inactivity.  The churchwardens supported these observations and added that they had often been subjected to criticism by irresponsible individuals, who never attended the meetings or helped forward in any way the cause they professed to uphold.  It was agreed that in future, a meeting of communicant members and others interested in the welfare of the church would be held every quarter.

For the rest of the register only Easter vestry meetings are recorded.  Subsequent meetings from 1895 mainly only elected churchwardens and sidesmen.  They were not very well attended; on one occasion only the vicar and wardens are recorded as being present.  There was one exception when in 1914 the field known as Church Headland Close and situated at the north end of the village at the junction known as Dean Turn was auctioned for letting, during the burning of a one inch (25mm) candle, to a Mr Chamberlain of Mill Farm for £1 0s 0d.  This field was let every year in the same way.  However, it was costing the church as much as, if not more than the rent to have the hedges cut and so it was decided that after the 1920 tenancy, future tenants would be responsible for cutting the hedges.  Some time later, in 1958, the field was sold to Mr Vincent of Mill Farm Nurseries. He also paid all expenses of the transfer which left a clear sum of £100 0s 0d available for charity. There was a hold up in selling the field, as there were no deeds. Mr Litchfield, one of the churchwardens, had to swear an affidavit to the effect that the field had belonged to the church for the past thirty years.

Not only were parishioners able to have a voice in the village through the Parish Council, they were given a voice in the running of the church as well. At the Easter vestry meeting in April 1922 the vicar, the Revd A S Dodds, explained the Parochial Church Councils (Powers) Measures Act. Communicant members of the church (about ten in number) were elected to stand on this new Parochial Church Council. They, with the vicar and churchwardens, were responsible for the running and upkeep of the church. From that time onwards the Easter vestry has only elected the churchwardens and sidesmen and gone straight on to the Annual Church Meeting. In effect two meetings in one. As a matter of interest the first lady churchwarden, a Mrs Jackson, was elected in 1903 and served for three years. This dual meeting was held in the evening at the school in Church Lane until 1986, when it moved to the new church room in the church. This arrangement changed again in 1995 when it became part of the Sunday morning service. In 1998 the responsibilities of the churchwardens were changed. One would be responsible for the church building and the other for the development and nurture of the congregation. In addition, a deputy warden was elected with responsibilities for record keeping. These posts would be re-elected annually, but now for a maximum of seven years.

**Free Seats for All**
Early in the 19th century the present nave was the north aisle and the chapel, now the church room, was the chancel. Work was carried out in the church in 1841-42 to provide extra seating. The plans were drawn up by William Farrar a carpenter and joiner from the parish. These were for re-seating and erecting a new gallery. The arches within the church were raised and the windows on the south of the church were heightened to let in more light. The work was carried out by William Farrar and Joseph Northern, a mason, at a cost of almost £250. A grant was made to the church by the Incorporated Church

All Saints Church - The People and their Building

*The chancel on the south side of the church* (*Photograph courtesy of Bedford County Archives*)

21

Building Society to help pay for the work. The church was reopened on 20 October 1842. A board to the left (west) of the church door records the event. It states that the new seats were free. Until then, those who could afford it paid for a pew in church and could expel anyone else using it, which as can be imagined would cause some embarrassment.

The Bedford Mercury of the 28 May 1842 reads, '. . . *at Riseley church, where two hundred exceeded the number of the congregation, the church is now filled to hear the same clergyman, and every one feels that he is not exposed to look about for an empty seat, from which he may be excluded on the coming of some solitary person to a large and empty pew, which takes up an undue portion of the church'*.

All this work nearly went to ruin when at the beginning of December 1875, during the morning service the roof caught fire. The vicar, the Revd J J Blick, had just got into the pulpit to deliver his sermon when one of the congregation raised the alarm. Immediately the vicar stopped the service and the churchwardens Messrs S Francis and J T Spencer, together with others, went up to the roof just as it burst into flames. With the aid of a few pails full of water the fire was put out. The cause was found to be an overheated stovepipe. Had the fire broken out between the services a great deal of damage would have been done.

**The Phoney Curate**
Scandal rocked the church in 1887. In February the Bishop of Ely, Lord Alwyne Compton, inducted the new vicar the Revd Edwin Giles. This was the first time an induction was made in public. The new vicar settled into Riseley very well taking a great interest in both the day school and Sunday School. He even introduced a children's service in church on alternate Sunday afternoons. Sadly he became seriously ill and a curate in charge, Revd W H Robins, was appointed. He lodged with Mr and Mrs Croot and entered into parish work with enthusiasm. However, early in October he went to London on what he called urgent business. He took with him a travelling rug belonging to the Croots and a watch belonging to their daughter (lent while his was supposed to be repaired). He did not return on the Saturday when he said he would and on investigation Mrs Croot found that he had taken all his

belongings. Although he had received his stipend he had not paid for the month's lodgings. It was later found that some books had been taken from the vicarage study and several blank cheques had been taken from the vicar's cheque book. One of these was made out for £18 and passed to Messrs Whipple & Co the clerical outfitters, to pay a small bill and the balance paid out to him in cash. It was later discovered that he had obtained a pair of boots from Mr Adams the boot maker in the parish and several Bedford tradesmen *'wanted'* him. Testimonies and references proved to be false, as was his name. His real name was Dent and he was not a real clergyman, but an impostor and a swindler. In November the vicar wrote a letter to The Times warning about clerical impostors. Mr Dent was not, as far as is known, caught. Early in December Revd Giles died leaving a wife and young family; even though he was only in Riseley a short time he was sadly missed.

The next vicar did not stay long either. The Revd Henry Longueville Graham, one of the clergy of Bournemouth St Peter, accepted the living in March 1888 and was inducted in April. In December the same year he resigned the living in Riseley to go to one in Hertfordshire which had become vacant due to the death of the incumbent, a friend of Revd Graham who wished Revd Graham to continue his work.

**Major Re-ordering in the Church**
When Revd John Ellis Turner came to Riseley from Christ Church, Luton, in March 1889, the church was in a sorry state. The area, which is now the chancel, was used as a kind of store with old benches, old pews, and other materials as well as housing the organ. It had been used as a school over 40 years before but it is thought that its condition became so unsafe the school was moved. The roof was in very poor condition, and the north aisle was made dark by the existence of the gallery, which was no longer used very much. On Ascension Day 1893 the ball was set rolling to restore the church to something of its former glory. Bazaars were held, collections taken and a subscription list opened to raise money. Working parties were held every week to clear the rubbish in order for the builders to start work. Whilst clearing out, some interesting remains were unearthed. In the wall between the chancel on the north side, and the chapel on the south side, a window was found of the early English style, blocked up with lathe and plaster.

Below it a very old and dilapidated piscina, used for washing the chalice and paten after communion, was found. Unfortunately, this was too badly damaged to repair and was replaced with a new one. In the same wall a squint was cleared out. This would have given a view of the ancient altar from the chapel. In the chapel itself a piscina and aumbry, used for storing the altar plate and other sacred items, were found under a double canopy. Messrs R Gell and Son of Bedford repaired the building and the architect was Mr Alfred Gotch of Kettering. The gallery was removed, as were the old square pews. The old rotten floor was taken up and replaced by pitch-pine blocks, and a new organ chamber was built. The altar was raised and the floor of the chancel and sanctuary paved with tiles. The cost of the work was about £250, but in addition to that a considerable amount was spent clearing out before the builders arrived. The building, which had been closed for some months, was formally re-opened on Wednesday 25 September 1895 by the Bishop of Ely, with a newly robed choir of 12 men and 12 boys under the direction of the organist Mr Packwood.

*The chancel on the north side of the church*

In the early part of the 20th century nothing major seemed to have happened either to or in the church. There had been a world war and sadly some from the parish had perished. A war memorial was erected in their honour. There is a note that in March 1933 the vicar Revd Reginald W E Robinson left after four and a half years. He was presented with a wallet containing five pounds. (Not bad considering that the deputy organist had been told at a meeting a few months earlier that there was no money to pay his fee of £3 a year.)

**A New Era**

*Reverend Paulson*

The Revd James C H Paulson came to the living in August 1933. Shortly afterwards, his father gave the church a carved oak priest's desk from a church in Portsmouth.

A great deal of work was carried out on the church building and in the parish, but the new vicar also introduced giving to missions both at home and overseas. The Christmas Day collections for that year went to the Church of England Waifs and Strays Society and the distressed area at Newcastle. To give people some idea of the Church's work overseas, lantern lectures about Africa were shown and missionary students welcomed. Over the next few years there were missionary weekends, exhibitions and festivals both in and around the parish. A Missionary Association was formed and in its first year concentrated on work in India. These were war years and the people of Riseley worked mainly on the land and incomes were low, yet people were generous with both their time and money. Some collections in church were given to the Red Cross for its war work. The church flourished numerically and spiritually, a Bible class for young men and boys was started and the Sunday School had between 60 and 70 children, the Mothers' Union was also well attended.

In 1937 responsibility for the chancel was taken over from the lay rector and patron, Lord St John of Bletsoe. This was not the present chancel but what was known as the Lady Chapel or St John Chapel (now the church room). The lay rector was responsible for keeping this portion of the church in good repair, but under the new tithe act it was to pass to the Parochial Church Council (PCC) after certain provision had been made by Lord St John. All defects were to be made good inside and out. Securities were to be invested to bring in a yearly income for repairs and a sum was to be invested to effect an adequate yearly insurance against fire. A surveyor carried out an inspection and estimated the cost of necessary repairs to be £194 7s 0d (£194.35).

In the summer of 1937 the Rushden Electric Supply Co was asked to submit an estimate for lighting the church. The cost of 13 lights in the church, Lady Chapel and vestry was to be £49 13s 3d (£49.66$^{1}/_{2}$). However, a piece of wood fell from the church roof giving some indication that work needed carrying out on the building. It was decided to ask Mr Cherry, an architect, to inspect the church and submit a report although later Mr Hughes of Cambridge took over the job. Meanwhile Messrs Taylors of Loughborough inspected the bells and tower. The roof, organ, heating, lighting, pinnacles and bells all needed attention, much of it urgent. The roof fund had £24 16s 4d (£24.82) in it. As these repairs needed a considerable sum of money, all church people were asked to have a collection box in their homes. The PCC also distributed a letter to every home as part of the appeal. The first objectives to be completed were the organ and a new Musgrove stove. The roof would take longer. As well as the boxes, the other events to raise money were whist drives, dances and carol singing. The Dramatic Society, of which the vicar was a member, also gave a generous donation from the proceeds of one of its shows. The Archdeacon suggested that copper be used on the roof instead of lead. The cost of the new copper roof was £1,551 but the allowance for the lead would be £1,404. This still did not include any timberwork, the estimated cost of which would be £2,700 plus architect's fees and any incidentals. The PCC *'pledged itself to go forward with the work'*. It was completed in 1952 at a cost of £4,500. Apart from £200 contributed by the diocese, the money had been raised in the parish. One parishioner made an interest free loan of £500; the vicar also made a loan of £250 – his stipend was £260 a year! In 1954 the PCC passed plans for electricity to be installed in the church. This was done in memory of Charles Henry Paulson, the vicar's father who had died in 1953. Due to ill health the vicar resigned on 10 January 1955. He presented a communion chalice and plate to the church. He had contributed much to the life of the parish and was greatly missed.

## All Saints Church - The People and their Building

*Reverend Davis*

On 29 September 1955, Revd Fredrick (Freddie) J C Davis was instituted as Vicar of Riseley. Due to poor attendance the vicar suggested that communion should be held at 9.30 am as a Choral Service. He re-formed the choir to include girls. In 1957 the church's patronage was transferred to The Martyrs' Memorial and Church of England Trust; although the transfer was generally agreed to, it was not welcomed at the time. The organ that until then had to be hand pumped by a choirboy, was fitted with an electric blower. Later, the organist's salary increased to 2s (10p) per service. By 1963 the old Musgrove stove had worn out and two Parkway oil fired air heaters were installed. In 1971 Taylors of Loughborough re-hung the peal of five bells. The old oak frame was removed and replaced by a steel girder cradle. A new treble bell, to make a peal of six, was installed in 1987 in memory of Thomas William Duncan, Constance Ella Duncan nee Barratt and Edith Ann Duncan (their daughter). Thomas Duncan had been the village policeman during the 1940s.

*Reverend Philips*

On the 28 March 1973 Revd Peter Philips became vicar of Riseley. He did not move into the vicarage, as it was large and difficult to heat in the winter, but moved into a house in Church Lane whilst the old vicarage was sold and a new one built on glebe land known as Cakebread Close. It was during the early part of his ministry that glebe land, that is land belonging to the church and rented out, which had until then been the responsibility of the incumbent, was taken over by the diocese. Later, on the 1 January 1979, Riseley All Saints and Bletsoe St Mary became a joint benefice. It was a time of change in the village with many new houses being built and young families moving into the parish. The choir was well attended and mastered the new music for the series three service as well as singing an anthem on special occasions and performing oratorios like Stainer's "Crucifixion" or Maunder's "From Olivet to Calvary" every year during Lent. Anthems were usually sung at the evening service at Easter and Harvest Festival. Another event that started at about this time was a joint service between the Anglicans and Methodists during Lent. This alternated between the church and chapel, starting on Ash Wednesday evening in church and finishing Maundy Thursday evening in the chapel. Lay people as well as clergy were invited to speak.

**Facing the Future**

*Reverend Bourne*

Revd David Bourne was inducted on the 10 September 1984. At about the same time a document "Facing the Future" came from the diocese. It invited churches to consider their position in terms of people and the building. This gave the church the impetus it needed to re-assess its situation and consider plans for the future. The Parish Magazine was re-organised to include Bletsoe, more village news and a summary of all village organisations. During 1985 various events were organised in the church. At about the same time the Sunday School was re-named CYPECS (Cypha, Pathfinders, Explorers, Climbers and Scramblers – the various stages: Scramblers being the youngest and Cypha, being the most advanced) and the annual holiday club for children was started in the church; it is held for a week in the summer holidays. More parents and children started going to church on a regular basis. Mission support was improved, the Children's Society, the Church Pastoral Aid Society and the Bible Churchman's Missionary Society (now called Crosslinks) were, and still are, supported. However, it became clear that after the church's quinquennial report (a survey carried out by the church architect), that a lot of work needed doing to the building. It was decided to link this work with some internal re-ordering and create a meeting room in what was then called the Lady Chapel. This would enable the children in CYPECS and another group called Omega, for older teenagers, to meet at the same time as parents attended the church service. The Friends of All Saints Trust was founded in 1985 to interest parishioners other than church members who were keen to see the parish church kept in good repair. Work was about to start when a piece of cornice fell from the ceiling in the chancel. On inspection the chancel roof was declared unsafe and the chancel closed. The altar was moved to the east end of the nave whilst work was carried out. A target of £65,000 was needed to carry out the necessary work. By September 1987 the church room was in use and paid for and by 1989 over £70,000 had been spent on repairs and improvements to the building. Despite all this work there was still not enough room for all age groups, in this growing church, to meet on Sunday mornings. The vicarage rooms were used to provide additional space. In 1992 work was carried out in the tower to create a new floor between the vestry floor and the bell-ringing chamber; this included a small balcony. The clock was removed from its position on the floor in the ringing chamber, cleaned, serviced and relocated on the wall and fitted with an electric winder. Until the winder was fitted, members of the church had taken it in turns to wind it daily.

In 1993-94 two steps were removed from the sanctuary, where the altar stands, the suspended wooden floors on which the choir pews stood were removed and a concrete floor laid flush with the tiles in the chancel (the choir having been disbanded). Whilst the chancel roof was being repaired, church members generally had grown to like gathering around the altar to take communion rather than kneeling in a row at the altar rail as they had done previously. When the altar was moved back into the sanctuary, a dais was built into the nave from the chancel step. The whole of the chancel and dais was carpeted and a temporary communion table was used until a permanent one was made by Phillip Nicholls, a Lay Reader. This enabled the chancel to be used by the music group on Sunday mornings or, fitted with chairs, for small or informal services. A sound system was installed by members of the church and updated in 2000. In 1986 new electric heaters had been installed in what is now the church room and in 1993 a completely new gas fired overhead heating system was put into the church.

*The chancel with dais and table*

Whilst work was carried out on the church building, missionary support was increased to support the training of Hilkiah Omindo, then a minister in the Anglican Church at Musoma, Tanzania. He is now the diocesan bishop. Two church members, Sue and Martin Fannon, spent three months in Musoma in 1999 and, after training, went to work there as missionaries in July 2000.

In 1986 the church started employing Careforce workers to help in the parish. Recognising the work to be done, the North Bedfordshire Christian Youth Trust was set up in 1996 and a full time youth worker, Roger Fawcett, came to work in churches and schools in the area. In 1998 Richard White was licensed as a Lay Reader.

Little mention has been made of the churchyard. All denominations except Quakers, who were buried in their own garden or orchard, have been buried there. In 1978 Marlene Gannon wrote a dissertation "The Use of Gravestones as an Historic Source" for her degree, and used All Saints churchyard for the study; it makes interesting reading. The oldest gravestone she found was of Ann Peacock dated 5 March 1691 aged 21 years. The youngest buried was 30 minutes old and the oldest 102 years. The most unusual burial was that of Frank Godfrey Sealey. Godfrey, as he was known, was born and lived in the parish all his working life; he had been a regular worshipper and had served on the PCC, but when he retired he and his wife moved to Bedford. It was only natural that when he died his wish was to have the funeral service and burial at Riseley. As the vicar was on holiday Godfrey's funeral service was taken by Revd Andrew Mottram, the vicar of Milton Ernest. As they came out of the church after the service, prepared for the burial, the undertaker hastily informed the vicar that they had sent the wrong coffin to the service and that Godfrey's had only just arrived. As far as is known, Godfrey is the only person buried in Riseley churchyard who was late for his own funeral.

*All Saints Church Riseley in the year 2000*

## Did you know that . . .

*Queen Katharine of Aragon is said to have stopped in Riseley in 1534. Following the annulment of her marriage to King Henry VIII she was imprisoned in various places around the country. It was while she was on her way from Ampthill to Kimbolton that she is supposed to have come through Riseley. While the horses were changed, she sat on a large stone, which was the base of an old Saxon Cross. The stone is still in place – opposite The Five Bells. Katharine died at Kimbolton Castle in 1536.*

*The famous stone on which Katharine of Aragon rested in 1534*

# The Moravians, Methodists and Baptists
Phillip Nicholls

**The Moravian Church** dates back to around 1415 when it was founded in Moravia, today part of the Czech Republic. The proper name for the Church is the 'Unitas Fratrum' or 'Unity of the Brethren'. It is only known by its nickname 'Moravian' in English speaking countries. The original Church suffered persecution during the counter reformation in the 16th and 17th centuries and survived as an underground fellowship over the next hundred years.

The present Church is dated from 1727 when refugees mainly from Moravia were granted permission to settle on lands belonging to Count Nicholas von Zinzendorf in Saxony, near the present border with Poland. Their intention had not been to establish a new Church but rather form societies within established Churches, to encourage work already going on. The aim was not realised for various reasons and a separate Church was formed.

*Moravian Chapel and congregation*

By 1741 the Moravians had established a settlement at Bedford St Peter. The congregation diary for November 1744 speaks of *'many being got together in Riseley'*. They preached here and in surrounding villages using private houses for their services. A Mr Woodward of Caldecot owned a house in Riseley, that he rented to them to hold services in 1745. John and Johanna Wade and their child, who lived with the Moravian community in Bedford, came to live in Riseley to take the services. He was liked very much by the villagers but there was clearly some jealousy from the parish church, as on 5 December the churchwardens had demanded his certificate *'pretty roughly'*. When he produced it and read it to them they had nothing to say. The Wades did not stay long as a letter from New York dated June 1747 sends greetings to Riseley.

In 1759 Robert Dawson and Robert Jackson produced and filed a certificate at Bedford Quarter Sessions, *'That the building lately erected on the west side of the High Street in the parish of Riseley . . . adjoining to an estate belonging to Mr Allen of Souldrop on the south and to another estate belonging to Mr Woodward of Caldecot on the north is a place appointed for holding and keeping Religious Meetings by those of his Majesty's Protestant subjects known by the name Unitas Fratrum'*.

There was a very strong connection between Bedford and Riseley as men used to come out from Bedford to take services. One such person was John Foster who lived at Brickhill; he drove his gig early on Sunday mornings along the coach road (A6) to Riseley. But others used to travel in the other direction. For example, on Good Friday 1780 four girls travelled from Riseley to Bedford for Easter. Only one, Sally Wain, is mentioned by name. They returned on Easter Day in the afternoon having attended services. Also, Mercy Warren's son wanted to move from Riseley into the choir house, or single brethren's house, in Bedford but unfortunately no employment could be found for him. From 1821 people were assigned to look after the congregation at Riseley, some were only here temporarily and others travelled to and from Pertenhall. The old chapel was demolished in 1810 and a new one built on the same site. In 1862 a new front was added. The new front had a door at both sides, the left-hand door was the men's entrance and the right-hand door the ladies'. The original windows were fitted at the sides. Riseley was unable to support its own minister as the people were poor and there was no endowment. The people only contributed to repairs and the upkeep of the Sunday School. It was not until 1889 that the suggestion was made to have a resident minister living in Riseley. The Eastern District Council (EDC) of the Moravian Church was to provide a house for him. Riseley was to become a home mission paid for by the EDC. The minister's salary was £60 a year. The village was thought to be a small but hopeful sphere of work.

By the end of the 19th century attendances were good; 58 in the Sunday School and up to 100 attending the evening service. By 1899 enough money had been raised for a new pipe organ. Although the attendance was good, there was an unwillingness to become a church member. At the beginning of the 20th century there was a flourishing branch of the Christian Endeavour Society. A name that crops up a lot about this time is Brother Schick. His parents had been in the West Indies, presumably as missionaries, when he was born. He became a missionary out there but on retirement came to look after the chapel in the village. Some villagers remember his daughters, Miss Schick and Mrs Brown living at 110 High Street.

Every year on the Sunday School anniversary there would be a special preacher. One year the Revd J P Porter came from London and another year the Bishop of the Moravian Church in England came. On the Monday a tent would be erected in a field belonging to Mr P H Banks for a tea party. In the evening there would be a service in the chapel and what seems like a lot of addresses (sermons). At one time the chapel had rooms for its social life opposite the old Methodist Chapel, where The Barns is now.

Unfortunately, whilst all was going well, at sometime in 1925 there came to the village Brother Osborne and his wife. He was a Rural Missionary on probation for the ministry. Nothing is known about him, except that in July 1926 he left without explanation to his wife or chapel committee. It transpires that he took with him the *'maypole money'* which had been collected whilst the children danced around the maypole.

Slowly the congregation declined. In the early 1940s temporary ministers were sent to the village, possibly due to the war. After this time three ministers came until 1961 when no new full time appointment was made. In 1963 Riseley was amalgamated with the Queens Park Church in Bedford and in 1966 the chapel closed.

For some time it was used to store furniture and later became the Chapel Gallery and remains so.

*Chapel Gallery, former Moravian Chapel, summer 2000*

**The Methodist Church** was founded by John Wesley. He was an Anglican clergyman who, while at Oxford, joined a group of friends calling themselves *'Methodists'* who sought to organise their lives according to strict standards of discipline, in contrast with society of the day. In 1736 he went to the new colony of Georgia trying to reproduce among the British settlers the kind of organised religion which he and his fellow Methodists had practised at Oxford. After two years he returned home a disappointed man. It was at a meeting with the Moravians in London that he experienced a turning point in his life. He and others travelled throughout the land on horseback preaching. He intended his people to follow his own example by attending the church services of the Church of England. They were to be supplemented not superseded, by simple Methodist preaching services at 5.00 am and 5.00 pm. These Methodists became increasingly reluctant to attend their parish churches and were in fact not always welcomed; Wesley himself was often forbidden to preach in churches. They increasingly established their own chapels and a complete pattern of their own Sunday services which, after the Plan of Pacification in 1795 included in nearly all places the Lord's Supper from time to time.

*The old Methodist Chapel - 1989*

During the last two decades of the 18th century, Wesley's helpers rode their large circuits to preach in a way that many had not experienced before. This presentation of the Gospel led to the conversion of two young men in Riseley. Although there was some opposition one of these men, Stephen Dickens, owned his own house which stood about where 131A High Street now stands, opposite Waldocks. He was able to open his home for Methodist worship without fear of a landlord's eviction, and there the first services were held. If the preacher was unable to travel from Bedford, the service would have been taken by someone in the village. It was also decided to meet every Sunday morning for prayer, and for many years there was a 7.00 am prayer meeting.

Later, in 1806, land was purchased from Joseph Farrar for the sum of £10 and in 1807 a chapel was built at the cost of £130. Originally Riseley was part of the Bedford Circuit but appears in the Higham Ferrers Circuit accounts book of September 1828 and on the Circuit Plan for the first quarter of 1832. A Sunday School was begun in the early 1820s and soon a larger building was necessary. In 1827 the building was extended towards the street, two windows were added, and a gallery was erected over the front door to accommodate the children. At the same time steps were built where previously there had been a path sloping up from the road.

As a result of this work there was a debt of £40, but as the chapel members were poor and interest had to be paid on the loan it remained for 40 years. In the end a special effort was made by Patty Simpson, who volunteered to collect one penny a week from members of the congregation. During the busy harvest season midweek services were suspended, but when they restarted a harvest tea was held to help clear the debt. In this way, over a period of years the debt was indeed cleared. When the money was paid, Daniel Rootham gave the railings by the steps and an iron fence. These stood until about 1942 when they were removed for war salvage. The zeal of the members seems to have waned shortly after this, possibly due to the debt, which had hung so heavily upon them. It was, however, revived by the preaching of an Anglican clergyman, the Revd T R Matthews, who had left his curacy in Colmworth to preach in the open air. He would arrive in the village on horseback and blow a huntsman's horn to call people together. A teenage girl, Mary Dickens, later Mary Bass, used to attend his meetings in Bedford walking both ways. However, as it was not possible to do this frequently, she and others who had been influenced by Revd Matthews found fellowship with the Methodists in Riseley. It is thought that his preaching was the cause of a revival in several Methodist chapels in the district.

The Methodist Sunday School had started about 1820 and in the Schedule for Chapels for 1851 the number of scholars attending was 60 in the morning, 60 in the afternoon and 55 in the evening. Like the

Moravians, the Methodist Sunday School anniversary was the great event of the year for the children. On the Monday there was the anniversary tea, followed by races and games and scrambling for sweets in a near-by field. It is recorded that in 1883, 383 people sat down to tea.

Mary Bass, nee Dickens, married in 1838 and became the mother of 12 children. The only education she had was in Sunday School where she learned to read and write.

Between 1850 and 1882 Methodism in Riseley was numerically at its height. The population of the village had increased from 576 in 1801 to 1,026 in 1861 (by 1901 it had decreased again to 735). The accommodation in the chapel in 1851 was 140 free seats and 73 others, and the average attendance that year was 33 in the morning, 92 in the afternoon and 106 in the evening.

The pews were family box pews, which were narrow and had high backs, each had a door fastened by a button. In the early days the singing was led by a clarinet or flute, and sometimes there were stringed instruments; later there was a seraphine (a cross between a piano and a harmonium). Hymns were read out two lines at a time for those who could not read very well. It is not known when the first organ was installed, but William Thornton and others collected for it sometime after 1872.

At the end of the 19th century work was carried out on the chapel, comfortable seats replaced the box pews and a wooden floor was laid. About the same time oil lamps replaced the candles. In 1911 it was necessary to renovate the building, the external walls were buttressed, internally seating near the pulpit was re-arranged and a new organ installed, the interior was painted. A new pulpit was needed in 1915 because of dry rot in the old one.

Local preachers turned out in all weathers to come to Riseley on Sundays. They took their preaching seriously, and one chapel member remembers, *'Our own Sunday seemed, like the Jewish Sabbath, to begin the evening before when most of the chores were done. It was a day of light, set apart for home, the family, books and that little chapel which brought us together at deeper levels'.*

In 1924 a young lay evangelist, David Edwards, came to Riseley to work in this and surrounding villages for a few months. He lived with Mr and Mrs Williamson. David gathered young and old together in a Wesley Guild. As at the turn of the century, the Moravian Christian Endeavour had been a centre of spiritual life for many young Methodists, so now Moravians joined the Wesley Guild. Under the leadership of Mr Williamson, this continued for 15 years and there are memories of lively discussion and good fellowship. In 1930 the chapel was registered for the Solemnization of Marriages. The first marriage was between Miss Nancy Harris and Mr John Neville.

The condition of the chapel became a problem and in 1938 the trustees resolved not to spend more on repairs but to build a new chapel with a schoolroom attached. No action was taken for several years and in 1940 it was decided to do nothing due to a lack of funds and war conditions. Electric lighting was installed in 1946 as was an efficient heating system, and in 1950 Mr North of Coldham Farm gave a new iron fence for the front of the chapel. In 1962 with a growing congregation and Sunday School, a vestry was made and toilet facilities were added.

Then an architect's report stated that the old chapel had to be rebuilt, having been considered unworthy of repair for 30 years. Also, there was a need for a room for the Sunday School as well as somewhere for the young people to meet after the evening service, or for weekday activities. With a growing village and an eye to the future it was decided that more space was required than the site in the High Street could offer. The decision was made to move on to the new estate off College Drive, and so a new building was erected in Wells Road. It was not only used for Methodist activities but by the village. For example, the play school used it until the new village hall was built.

Unfortunately, as the years went by membership of the chapel decreased, but the faithful few still meet and give a warm welcome to anyone who joins them.

The Moravians, Methodists and Baptists

*The old Methodist Chapel which was virtually dismantled and is now a private house*

*The new Methodist Chapel*

**The Particular, or Strict Baptists**, are Calvinistic. They are conservative in theology, make their decisions as a congregation and stress the priesthood of all believers. Allowing full participation in every aspect of the life and work of their chapels, they also stress the separation of church and state.

*The Baptist Chapel on the corner of Keysoe Road and High Street*

At the beginning of the first and only minutes book of the Riseley Baptist Chapel we read: *'In the spring of 1838 the Father of Mercies gave to a few of his numerous family an ardent desire to introduce the gospel in its purity and simplicity into Riseley, a benighted village containing a thousand inhabitants'*. A small number of like-minded Baptists had been meeting in Riseley but the place where they met had fallen into decay and they looked for alternative accommodation. They approached Mrs Everit of The Five Bells for the use of a large barn that stood on her premises. It was there that they, and some others from Sharnbrook, held their first meeting on 1 June 1838. The preacher was the Revd John Peacock of Goswell Street, London. As the congregation increased over the next few months a committee was formed for the purpose of purchasing a piece of land on which to build a Meeting House. Land was purchased at the corner of the High Street and Keysoe Road and building commenced. After they had been meeting in the barn for about four months, the days were shortening and the evenings were getting cold, so they met within the walls of the Meeting House.

When the building was nearly finished they held their first service on Wednesday 3 October. The next year on Wednesday 27 February they formed a Christian Church of the Particular Baptist denomination. Mr S Beall of Bletsoe Park was elected as the first deacon; in 1840 a second deacon, Mr Slaney was appointed. The chapel started with 11 members, and on 24 June Mr W Flanders became the first pastor. He was publicly ordained to the pastoral charge of the church on the 2 July. Although all were made welcome at their services, the Baptists were very strict as far as church membership was concerned. If anyone wanted to join the church, two existing members visited them to enquire of their spiritual welfare. The members then reported back to the church and if they approved the individual was *'encouraged to come forward at the next Church Meeting and declare what God had done for their souls'*. If a member of their church moved into or out of the village then they had to get an honourable dismission from the chapel they were leaving before they could be admitted into full communion with their new chapel. Any who joined had to undergo baptism by total immersion; the first members at Riseley had to go to Staughton. After a while, a baptistery was built inside Riseley chapel which, when used was filled with water from the brook. The water was carried to the chapel by means of a steam engine towing a water bowser.

At the Church Meeting in September 1841 it is recorded that Mr Slaney, one of the deacons, after being ill for some time exhibited the symptoms of insanity. Friends watched over him but at the Sunday Meeting on 8 August he slipped away. It was not until the following Tuesday that Mr Lugsdin's shepherd found him drowned. He was sadly missed by his chapel friends.

Encouraging people to become members of the chapel was not easy but if any member erred and did not repent they were *'separated from their communion'*. It is noted that, *'a report having been in circulation of an unpleasant nature respecting Eliza Swannel, and such report having been confirmed, the church was of an opinion that they must come to the painful necessity of separating her from their communion'*. What could she have done? Members were only usually dismissed through lack of attendance.

After Mr Flanders had left a Mr Wallis became pastor in 1843. The next year the first deacon Samuel Beall died. He had been a faithful servant of the chapel. Mr Wallis did not stay long, as in August 1847 Mr Dickerson of London became pastor. In 1859 Mr W Wilson became pastor. It is reported that attendance was good – in fact the chapel was often packed. Lanternslide lectures were given during the week, one was on Pilgrims Progress at which the Revd Cook of the Moravian Chapel presided. Another on Canada and the North West was given by the Revd T G Head of Keysoe, who had recently returned from Canada.

*The green where the Baptist Chapel used to stand*

In 1889 improvements were carried out in the chapel; a bazaar was held to raise money. Fixed lamps replaced the candlesticks, a new pulpit was erected and wooden boards replaced the bricks on the floor of the pews. After Mr Wilson left in 1867 there were other pastors but the zeal seems to have gone. After 1863 there are only a few meetings minuted until 1929 when it was reported that there were no male members left to carry on the services. Edwin Rootham of Kettering preached on Sundays until 1948 when it was decided to terminate the cause and close the chapel which, with the agreement of the Charity Commissioners was sold for £255. The invested interest (proceeds from the sale of fields adjoining), was by order of the Charity Commissioners diverted to the Strict Baptist Chapel at Sharnbrook, as being the nearest chapel of the same faith to Riseley.

Shortly afterwards the chapel was pulled down allowing the road to be widened. The only sign that there was once a place of worship there are some gravestones which remain.

Although each of the Christian organisations went its own way, there were times when they united, and nothing unites more than outside intrusion. In August 1885 two American preachers belonging to The Seventh Day Adventists pitched a tent capable of seating 250 people in Pool (now Ross) Meadow. Meetings supporting their view were held each evening. The main point they made was the observance of Sabbath keeping on Saturday and not Sunday; the village was divided on the question.

The following Sunday Mr Fountain of Sharnbrook preached a *'masterly discourse'* in the Baptist Chapel in support of Christian Sabbath observance, at which the Americans were present. They replied to his sermon on the Monday challenging anyone to disprove them. A Mr Pierson, possibly the headmaster of the village school, accepted the challenge on the following Thursday evening, but exception was taken to his not being a minister. The religious assembly broke up amidst a scene of disorder and confusion.

Happily, there were other occasions when all met together. Perhaps the best remembered were the Harvest Festivals. As the village was, by and large, a farming community it is not surprising that the church and chapels supported each other, the Harvest Season ending with a large communal service in the parish church.

## *Did you know that . . .*

*Tom Knocker's Pond, by the side of the road from Bletsoe to Riseley, is haunted by the ghost of Tom Knocker who drowned there years ago. Tom was an itinerant farm labourer and he was found face down in the pond one day by a fellow worker, who dragged the body out of the pond and raised the alarm. When he returned to the pond with reinforcements, Tom's body was once again face down in the water. It is rumoured that his ghost can be seen on the road near to the pond.*

*The Fox and Hounds is haunted by a nurse, killed in an accident. Some time in the 19th century, she slipped from a coach and was trampled by the horses. She was taken to The Fox and Hounds, which was the nearest inn, where it is rumoured that her ghost can still be seen.*

*If you walk around the church 12 times just before midnight on hallowe'en and then look up at the gargoyle above the main door, it will spit at you!*

# The Village School
## Julia Jarman

Riseley Voluntary Aided Lower School was built in 1841, 30 years before local authorities were compelled to provide schools for the poor. From the start it was a Voluntary Aided school, set up and run by the church, aided by government grants. Church schools proliferated during the 19th century, part of a widespread religious revival.

Some children *'went to school'* in the village even before the school was built in Church Lane. As early as 1610, there was a teacher in Riseley. We know of Thomas More, who would have taught some of the villagers to read the Bible. By 1818 there was one Sunday School and three or four day schools in Riseley. By 1833 there was one day school *'with 27 males and 3 females'*, probably held in the church. We know there was a *'school'* in the chancel till 1841. There were also two Sunday Schools in the village, one run by the Church of England, the other by the Methodists. The Moravians educated their own children.

It is clear that a number of Riseley parents wanted their children, particularly their boys, to have some schooling - to learn to read and write perhaps and escape the poverty they endured, or to learn about God. Some may have wanted a few hours respite from their large families, but, whatever their motivation, these parents valued school enough to send their children to school and pay the *'school pence'*. School attendance wasn't compulsory until 1880. It wasn't free till 1891.

We know what motivated the school founders. They saw it as their Christian duty to improve the lives of the poor, especially their morals. So when the church roof became unsafe and the school couldn't continue there, a purpose built school was planned.

It was to be called The National School and National meant Church of England. The trust deed makes it clear that the school was *'to be used for the education of children and adults or children only of the labouring and other poorer classes in the said Parish of Riseley . . . in the principles of the Established Church'*.

Riseley – Our Village

To qualify for grant aid, the government insisted on a conscience clause giving dissenters the right to opt out of Religious Instruction. Religious Instruction had to take place at the beginning or end of the school day so that dissenters could absent themselves easily.

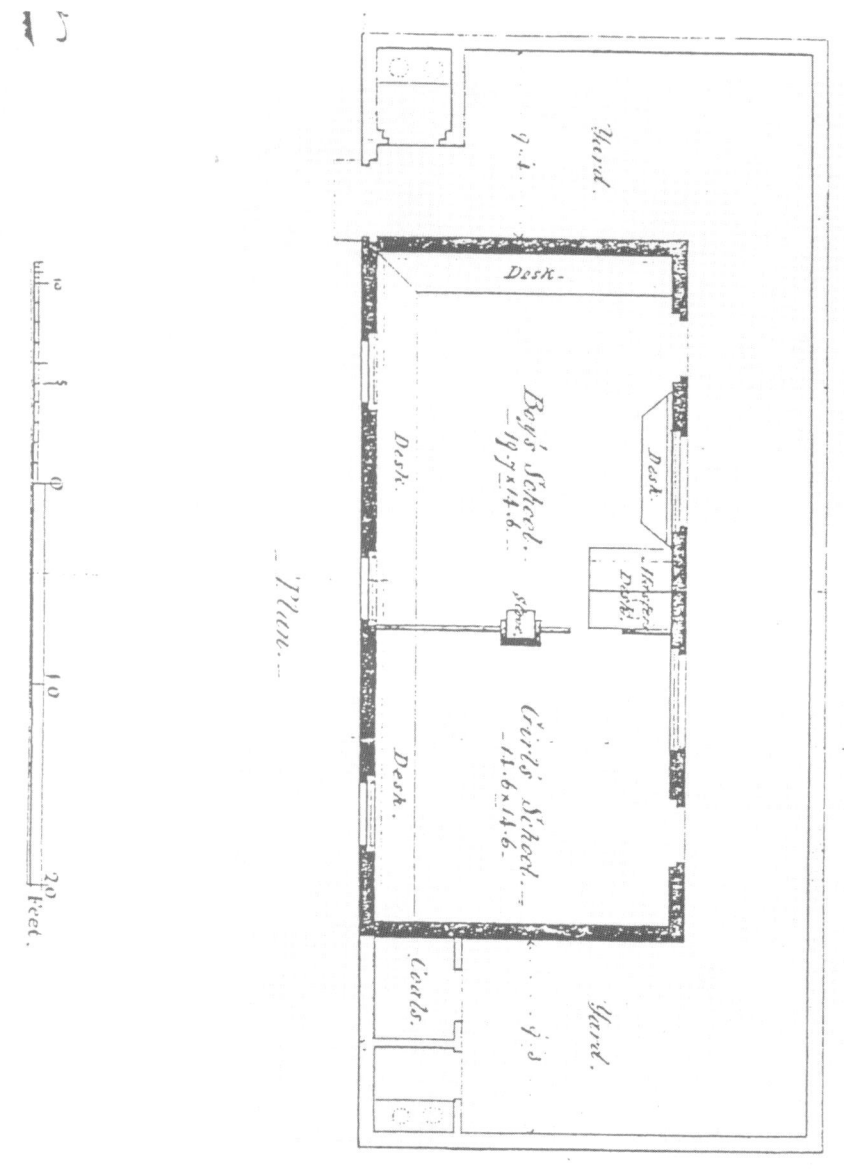

The School as shown on the original architect's plan (copied from slides held by the County Records Office)

It was a school for the poor – the rich sent their children away to school or educated them at home – but the rich helped with the costs. Lord St John, who lived at Melchbourne, gave £113 for the building, which was on his land. This building now houses the staff room, the headteacher's study and the secretary's office. Originally thatched, it consisted of one large room, divided into two sections one for boys, one for girls. There was a stove in the middle, on the side near the road, and the teacher sat near it. Records for 1846-47 show that there was a master and a mistress and that 30 boys and 32 girls attended on Sundays and weekdays. The increase in the number of girls is interesting. From 1848 the master lived in schoolhouse, built when Lord St John donated more land.

*The School as shown in the original architect's plans and drawings (copied from slides held by the County Records Office)*

By 1848 pupil numbers were increasing, though the village population was falling at this time. Education was catching on. Another classroom was needed and half the present school hall was built, doubling the total area. Many children would have seen their fathers or elder siblings working on the School House or the new extension, but not from the classroom windows, which were small and high up the walls. In 1871 the school was extended again, for more pupils, this time because the Education Act of 1870 made provision of schools compulsory.

From 1871 the master and the managers kept logs so we have detailed records of events as they saw them. On 30 May 1871 the managers met *'to consider what must be done to meet the requirements of the late Act for the Education of the poor'*. They noted that the population of Riseley was 1,028 – about 200 households – and estimated that 15 families would not use the school. (Moravians tended to educate their own children, though the Moravian minister was one of the school managers; many girls attended the lace schools where they could earn and learn a trade; some children may have gone to *'dame schools'* because they were cheaper or warmer.) Managers calculated that 190 children must be accommodated, and anticipated an increase of 55. So, the other half of the present school hall was built.

Money – for the building and day to day running – was a concern right from the start. Government grants were available but could not be relied upon because the system was Payment by Results. The grant depended on satisfactory attendance figures, test results and reports from the dreaded inspectors. The managers raised funds by subscriptions and by rates. A record for 1871 shows that the sum of £35 11s 6d (£35.57$\frac{1}{2}$) raised was spent on desks, blackboards and maps, and the carriage of the desks.

These items help us picture the classrooms. But what were those maps used for? Geography was not on the syllabus yet. Were they to show children the extent of the British Empire or where missionaries were working to convert the heathen?

In August 1871 there were 145 on roll – 86 boys and 59 girls – an increase of ten not the predicted 55. There was still some resistance and some families couldn't afford the *'pence'*, though the rate varied according to income.

> 104 pupils paid 1d each per week.
> 32 pupils paid 2d each per week.
> 6 pupils paid 4d each per week.
> 3 pupils paid 6d each per week.

This raised 210d per week, (17s 6d, 87$^1$/2p in today's money). It formed part of the master's salary, which he had to negotiate himself. It was often a matter of contention. In 1872, Mr Pierson agreed an annual salary of £42, *'together with the whole of the school pence and the Government grant subject to a deduction of one half of the pupil teacher's salary'*. I estimate this totalled around £120, a large sum compared with other earnings in the village. But for this he had to run the school, teach pupils six days a week and train the pupil teachers in his own time. When he stopped helping with the Sunday School, managers deducted £2 and also decided that if he had the manure for his garden, the expense of cleaning out the closet was to be paid by him!

Money never stopped being a worry for the managers who found it difficult to remain solvent. They wanted children of parents on Parish Relief to come free – Mr Pierson disagreed – but found they couldn't afford this idealism. So when compulsory attendance became law in 1880 they had another worry, Attendance Officers. But how could they make paupers send their children to school and pay for it?

Staffing was another problem. The rapid expansion of education led to a shortage of trained teachers, but Mr Pierson himself stayed for 16 years. Eventually a disagreement over money made him leave. In 1886 Inspectors withheld the government grant because the fabric of the building did not reach prescribed standards. They criticised the dingy, dirty state of the classrooms, too cold in the winter, stiflingly hot in the summer. *'The infants are taught in a dingy room, poorly fitted up, with a brick floor and defective apparatus.'*

The managers asked the master to agree to a reduced salary. He refused and left. According to the vicar it was the loss of a *'first rate man'*.

By all accounts Mr Pierson was an effective man who built up attendance figures, strove hard to reach government attainment targets – and had a strong sense of his own worth. It was difficult trying to please all parties. The official Inspectors required children to reach standards in the 3 Rs. The Diocesan Inspector required them to be familiar with the Bible, the catechism and the Christian year, and to know by heart several scriptures, psalms, hymns and collects! Mr Pierson complained, *'. . . a great deal too much is expected and it seems to me superfluous to teach the liturgy of the Church of England, in a school composed very largely of dissenting parents'*.

The managers agreed with him but on 15 October 1874 they observed, *'that during the last fortnight or three weeks, by Mr Pierson's order, the Bible has not been read in school'*. He was told, *'that he was on no account to omit such reading of the Bible'*.

By the 1880s the vicar was helping with Religious Instruction, but Mr Pierson still had a lot to do. A whole army of inspectors could drop in at any time. They included the vicar and other managers, the Diocesan Inspector who tested religious knowledge, the official Inspectors, who could criticise anything from the 3 Rs to hygiene and, from 1876, Attendance Officers.

In 1883 Riseley was praised because attendance had increased more than in any other school in the district! In her fictional portrait of Riseley in the 1880s Mary Frampton writes: *'Parents marvelled at the wonderful arithmetical knowledge of their progeny and their quickness in the matter of ascertaining change'*. This may have been true, but frequent absences still hindered progress. There were times when parents wanted children to help at home or in the fields. At harvest time attendance dropped so low that the Head sometimes closed the school. This was the origin of our long summer holiday. Mr Pierson recorded absences in the logbook. Note that at this time the total roll was between 150 and 190.

*Aug 4th 1870*   *Only 20 present, all gone into the harvest fields.*
*Sept 12th 1870*   *Potato digging is causing many to be absent.*
*Oct 14th 1870*   *24 present in morning: only 14 in afternoon. Several having gone picking acorns.*

*June 25th 1875*   *Attendance this week lower than last the haymaking season having set in.*
*July 6th 1877*   *Several scholars absent this week, being engaged carrying meals to their friends in the hayfields.*
*Mar 8th 1878*   *Several boys were absent at work in the fields crow-scaring and weeding.*
*July 16th 1881*   *The remaining scholars were absent pea-pulling.*
*Oct 21st 1881*   *On Thursday the number went down considerably, some being absent to pick potatoes, others to gather acorns and others to gather wood broken off by the late strong winds.*

A picture emerges of a rural community in which school was welcomed by most of the parents – records don't show what the children thought – unless it conflicted with basic needs. But there was a hard core of parents who kept their children at home or sent them elsewhere. Many girls went to the lace-making schools in the village. This caused problems for Mr Pierson.

*Sept 20th 1870*   *Ascertained that Eliza Nutter had gone to learn lace-making.*
*Nov 20th 1874*   *The Factory Inspector came to school on Friday afternoon to enquire about those who made lace and did not attend school. On Monday morning had a great influx of half-time girls from the Lace schools.*

The weather also affected attendance. When heavy snow caused men to be laid off work, there was no money for school pence. Many children did not have outdoor clothes to protect them in extreme weather. Violent winds and especially rain often caused absences and sometimes the closing of the school. Past and present day pupils may recognise the following situation.

*Jan 1877*   *Wednesday afternoon was very wet but 72 presented themselves and were marked. After having had one lesson their friends came for them in order to get them home before the water got too high, as the brook was overflowing rapidly and causing a flood . . . Some of the scholars were fetched away in a cart as the water was too deep for them to wade through.*

Riseley – Our Village

We can imagine the cheers that greeted this early exit from school, a grim place in many respects in the 19th century. Conditions did improve after the Inspector's report which led to Mr Pierson's departure. A raised platform called the gallery was built to enable the teacher to keep an eye on the youngest children.

The Inspectors commented:
*'1888   The classroom is greatly improved by the new gallery, and would be made more attractive by the addition of a few pictures.'*

Inspectors tried hard to push up standards, and possibly keep down the government grant. But things quickly got worse again.

*'1890   The stove has been out of order all winter and the room in consequence imperfectly warmed. The walls need re-colouring and the woodwork repainting.'*

*'1894   So intensely cold today that the ink was frozen in the inkwells and it was almost impossible for the children to hold their pens.'*

Poor children! Chilblains and blisters were another problem, caused by the cold and by ill-fitting shoes. Clothes were often hand me downs. Pupils were often suffering by the time they reached school, where they had to bundle wet clothes under their benches.

Sanitation at home and school was bad - so it's not surprising that infectious diseases kept children off school and sometimes caused it to be closed completely. Many logbook entries note epidemics of sickness, coughing and diarrhoea. In the 19th century ringworm is mentioned but not head lice. Was it too common to report or were Riseley children amazingly immune from this infestation so common in Victorian times? The primitive lavatories often caused comment. Situated at either end of the oldest building – girls at one end, boys at the other - they gave out a disgusting smell particularly in hot weather.

*Jan 1871         Noise made by coughing drowns every other noise.*
*Jan 1880         The school was closed by the Sanitary Inspector owing to Scarlet Fever being in the Schoolhouse. During the said two*

|   |   |
|---|---|
| | *weeks the school rooms were well fumigated with brimstone and limewashed.* |
| *Dec 1881* | *Measles being so prevalent the school was closed by Sanitary Authority from Monday Dec 12th to Friday Dec 30th.* |

Illness affected the staff too and not only in winter.

|   |   |
|---|---|
| *June 1882* | *The teacher A Litchfield absent the whole week from sore throat and a great bodily weakness, caused by cold and over exertion.* |

It also affected the staff's families. Scarlet fever in School House caused the school to close in 1880. On several occasions the master's children are described as *'dangerously ill'* and the master's wife, who was expected to help teach whether she was qualified or not, had to take time off to tend to her sick children. Infant mortality was high and there are several mentions of children dying and being taken to the mortuary.

Good old days! The records completely dispel a rosy-eyed view of the past. It's hard to say who was more miserable, the children or the teachers. Teachers were strict but poor discipline was a problem, mentioned by the first Head, Mr Peake and all others afterwards.

|   |   |
|---|---|
| *Oct 17th 1870* | *School is most unsatisfactory, discipline very bad.* |
| *Jan 26th 1871* | *Several scholars who came late made to stand by themselves on a bench for punishment.* |
| *Feb 17th 1871* | *Punished a first class boy for repeated lying by making him stand on a stool in the corner of the room with a placard pinned to his back on which was printed the word LIAR in large letters.* |

Mr Pierson, the second Head, complained about the lack of discipline when he first came.

|   |   |
|---|---|
| *Sept 27th 1872* | *Find that some of the scholars in the first class are in the habit of taking advantage when my eye is not on them.* |

He is still complaining 11 years later.

*Jan 11th 1883*   *A third standard scholar dipped his fingers in the ink and deliberately rubbed it across a new geographical reader, for which he received four strokes on the hand. He seems to be a naturally troublesome boy.*

In and out of school, boys would be boys it seems and that meant rough play. Even the policeman's son got into trouble:

*Jan 29th 1874*   *It was decided that King the policeman should be responsible for repairing a panel in the new door at the school – which had been kicked in by Henry King, Alfred Bailey, Frederick Gell and John Roberts, leaving it to him to discover how far the other three boys were really implicated and to obtain from their parents a fair and just share of the expenses.*

Playtimes were particularly unruly. There are a lot of reports of bullying and violence. The following are typical:

*Nov 1880*   *Two scholars quarrelled and one knocked the other, so that he could not stand, but had to be taken home in a perambulator.*

*June 1892*   *Punished Thomas Packwood for interfering with the school lamps and for stinging a little boy with nettles during play hour.*

When Mr Pierson left the next two masters stayed only two years each. Perhaps insolence from pupil teachers hastened their departure. One teacher, Miss Towblin, gave both headteachers, cause for concern.

*Feb 1889*   *Miss Towblin, late at morning school (25 minutes) Master spoke about it and she was very insolent.*
*Jan 1890*   *The object lesson on A Letter by Miss Towblin was a complete failure. The Master gave the lesson afterwards and once more insisted on preparation of work.*

'Object lessons' were introduced towards the end of the century, in a bid to make the syllabus more interesting and relevant, so that behaviour would improve perhaps. For most of the 19th century a normal day started with Morning Prayers and Religious Instruction and was followed by the 3 Rs. Copying from the board and rote learning were the main methods. Singing was also part of the compulsory curriculum and for the girls there was sewing. Sewing was taught by the master's wife and Inspectors frequently criticised the low standard of dressmaking. While the girls did sewing – or knitting in the charge of the rebellious Mrs Sumner who was reprimanded for her initiative in 1890 – the boys did more of the 3 Rs! Later, in the 1890s geography was put on the syllabus – for boys – while the girls did sewing. Then geography was taken off and singing substituted.

Singing may have provided some light relief but there is no evidence of pleasure in the records we have. There is no mention of sport or games. Nor is there any record of stories being told or read to the children. There seems to have been nothing on the syllabus designed to engage or stimulate the imagination. Object lessons – on camels and elephants if not boots and shoes – may have broadened mental horizons. They were made compulsory for younger children in 1895 and continued into the 20th century. The example overleaf shows that teachers were shown both what and how to teach. In the method the teacher is told exactly how to proceed.

These lessons could be interesting, especially if models or pictures were used, but in the hands of some teachers they became sterile question and answer sessions. Miss Towblin wasn't the only unsatisfactory teacher. Headteacher, Mr Rowlands records:

*Oct 1888*  *Heard Miss Blott give a model lesson on Boots and Shoes . . . she was told that she would have to try and make the lesson more interesting so as to secure both attention and discipline.*

Again and again records report a new master's denunciation of the low standards of attainment and behaviour that he finds in the school. Pupils were subjected to frequent tests in an effort to raise standards and raise awareness of problem areas. Ever so many visitors and teachers over the years commented on the *'extreme backwardness'* of the pupils. (Like many rural counties Bedfordshire was considered backward with 51% literacy, compared with 88% in London and 81% in Northumberland, a rural county, which had a reputation for good education.) Records also show masters leaving, usually after only a

NOTES OF LESSONS ON FAMILIAR OBJECTS.

## THE CAMEL.

### MATTER.

**I. Where found.**

Camels are found in Central and Northern Asia. There are two kinds, the Arabian, or one hunched, camel or dromedary, and the Bactrian, having two hunches.[1]

**II. Description of the Camel.**

(a) HEIGHT. About 8 feet.
(b) COLOUR. Dark brown, inclining to red.
(c) TEETH. Very similar to those of a dog.
(d) STOMACH. The arrangement of the camel's stomach is very peculiar. Its food passes into one portion, while the other contains a large supply of pure water which it can drink at pleasure.[2]
(e) BACK. Some naturalists say that the hump on the camel's back disappears to supply it with food, and that when the body has been once more restored to its proper state, it returns.[3]
(f) LEGS AND FEET. Both well adapted to its mode of life. Its knees and feet are provided with elastic-like cushions.[4] Its feet are partly cloven.[5]

**III. Habits.**

Camels will not tread upon marshy ground if they can avoid it, hence their masters are sometimes bound to spread for them their tent coverings in order to induce them to proceed. They chew the cud[6] and are very vicious towards each other, camel fights being of frequent occurrence.

They feed principally upon thorny shrubs, date leaves, and beans.[7]

**IV. Uses.**

(1) *When alive.*
  (a) As a beast of burden. It will travel 5 or 6 miles per hour with a load of 300 lbs.[8]
  (b) Milk. A favourite beverage, that of the sheep and goats being made into butter.
(2) *When dead.*
  (a) Flesh. Cut up and salted for food.

### METHOD.

The last animal we spoke of was one living in very cold countries. To-day I wish to talk to you about one living in hot climates. What do you think it is called? The Camel.

[1] The latter is the true camel; that with one hunch is generally known as the dromedary.

[2] Here shew its adaptation to desert life.

[3] Probably this is fiction.

[4] By this arrangement it is enabled to kneel comfortably when being laden.

[5] Comp. the llama's, &c.

[6] Comp. the cow.

[7] The Arabs in providing for a long journey pound the date stones, and then feed their camels upon a kind of cake made by mixing this flour with water.

[8] More than two cwts. (In an upper class let this sum be worked.)

*A page from an 'Object Lesson' of 1897*
*(copied from slides held by the County Records Office)*

couple of years, having failed to improve standards. Mr Sumner was another who left when managers reduced his salary. Masters often left feeling unappreciated. But in 1891 Mr Hewitt arrived and stayed for 31 years! He stayed till 1922 and led the school into the 20th century. Quite soon a *'modern'* note is struck when Mr Hewitt questions the need for so many academic tests!

*April 30th 1897 . . . I find such frequent tests are a great waste of valuable time which might be more profitably employed in teaching and they moreover entail a great deal of unnecessary labour upon the teacher.*

In 1897 he logged the following year's lessons and we see that the syllabus covers a broader range of subjects now.

*1897-8*
*Standards 1 and 2. Growth of a plant from seed. Wool, cotton, flax, clay, iron, coal, salt.*
*A road, cow, sheep, horse, camel, reindeer, elephant.*
*The four seasons, clouds, silk, paper, an egg, life history of a butterfly, propagation of plants.*

But from now on we can see the school from another angle. We can draw on the memories of local residents, several of whom born early in the 20th century, remember Mr Hewitt.

Mrs Bates, born 1900, and formerly Mabel Chamberlain, was a pupil at Riseley School from 1905 to 1914 when she left aged 14. She returned as a teacher in 1919. Speaking in 1991 she vividly remembered her days as a pupil.

*'The Headmaster was Mr Hewitt and his wife Mrs Hewitt was also involved with the school. She used to teach household management. She applied a practical approach to her teaching and used to take the children into School House where they learnt how to clean windows, sweep and wash floors and other domestic chores.'*

Mrs Bates remembered Mrs Hewitt, *'a large lady'* once coming into class and sitting on a carpet chair that collapsed beneath her. She ended up lying flat on the floor. Everyone laughed and she sent several boys to her husband for the cane. She doesn't seem to have been popular despite her *'delicious mince pies, flaky pastry and deep fried doughnuts'* which she baked with the pupils. They could buy the baking to take home. Mrs Bates comments that when the Hewitts retired a collection was made but *'several people refused to contribute because they thought Mrs Hewitt had been too much of a disciplinarian'*.

Mrs Bates, then Miss Chamberlain, returned to Riseley as a teacher in 1919. As in the 19th century, *'the children formed fours and drilled before marching into school'*. Morning Assembly, in which she played the piano, was another daily feature. Lessons were varied, she records, but emphasis was placed upon the 3 Rs. The children were taught phonics and their reading books were *'a German reading scheme'*, which sounds extraordinary and not completely effective. To encourage reluctant children Mrs Bates used to cut out a comic strip called Teddy Tales from the Daily Mail. *'The children loved these.'*

Miss Waldock, born 1907, was another pupil who became a teacher at the school. She started school when she was 4 and left when she was 11 to go as a boarder to the Girls Modern School in Bedford. Sitting in the *'gallery'* aged 4 or 5 is her earliest memory of the school. She remembers a Scripture lesson with the children *'quarrelling about who would get to the top row'*. In 1912 the gallery was removed by Mr W Litchfield and a new

*One of the earliest woodwork classes, showing young Stanley Litchfield at the front bench and probably the headmaster Mr Hewitt*

cooking range was fitted where the gallery used to be, for the use of cookery classes at evening school or during the daytime.

Practicality was the innovative feature of the 20th century, to engage boys like steam enthusiast, Bert Curtis perhaps. At school in 1918 he *'preferred to join the threshing gang rather than sit in school'*. He remembers the traction engines trundling up Gold Street, then a rutted grass way, but not a lot about school! Woodwork for boys was introduced in 1911 and gardening was on the syllabus by 1916.

There was some continuity from the 19th century of course. The Victorian attitude of *'Spare the Rod and Spoil the Child'* was still prevalent. The school day still began with religious worship, emphasis was still on the 3 Rs. Miss Waldock's memories of the early 20th century echo reports of much earlier times.

She remembers the classroom as very dark and badly ventilated with small high windows. *'It accommodated children between three and 13 years. It was so cramped that the children found it hard to move. They squeezed on to forms as tightly as they could. There would have been about 100 children in the school at the time. They often took time off to go potato picking, gleaning corn, picking up acorns to feed the pigs, scaring birds, pea-picking and gathering cowslips and dandelions for their mothers to make wine. There was no playground and the children played in the Lane.*

*A bell summoned the children to school morning and afternoon. There was a bell tower on the end of the hall. There was a little hole in the roof with a chain and a rope at the end. At a quarter to nine the first bell would ring. Everyone in the village could hear it. On Empire Day the children would walk in procession to the church, salute the flag on the church tower, sing the National Anthem then return to school, where they were given a half-day holiday. They didn't go into the church.'*

The Head's log for Empire Day, 24 May 1922 records the full programme for the day and shows that respect for King and Country was an important part of the curriculum.

Miss Waldock also remembers Mrs Hewitt's practical approach. *'One day we had to clean the bedroom, polish the furniture and make the bed.'* On another day she took them into the kitchen. *'She was going to have the teachers to tea and she wanted to show us how to lay a table. She scrambled eggs and made egg and cress sandwiches.'* Like Mrs Bates she also remembers Mrs Hewitt's harsher side. *'We had to knit twine and I couldn't get the needle to go through so I said, "Please Ma'am"* – we always called her Ma'am –*"I can't push the needle through". She told me off and hit me on the arm with a ruler.'*

Miss Waldock became a teacher whom everyone remembers with affection. She taught the *'babies'* or Reception class from 1926 to 1973. She had no formal training after leaving the Girls Modern School when she was 16 but took to teaching *'like a duck to water'* when the Vicar asked her parents if she could help them out of a difficulty, when the previous teacher left to get married. *'I loved the children. Inspectors came, very grim, but they always said, "You're doing fine. Carry on doing what you're doing." '*

It's interesting to note that a school photograph of 1927 is the first in which the children – and the teacher – are smiling. Photographs before that date show serious, worried even suspicious expressions.

An earlier photograph from around 1890 looks as if it was taken on some special occasion, Empire Day perhaps? The children seem to be wearing their best clothes. The girls are not wearing the pinafores they would have worn on ordinary days. Many of them wear beautiful lace collars. Several boys sport flowers in their buttonholes. Maybe having a photograph taken was cause enough for celebration but no one looks happy! Who are the teachers in this photo? The dapper man with the quiff and the well-upholstered woman are Mr and Mrs Hewitt who were there from 1891 to 1922. Their own children stand next to them.

Mrs Bates and Miss Waldock, pictured in both the 1927 and the 1951 photographs, do seem to have had a different attitude from their predecessors. Certainly Miss Waldock's gentle personality was a contrast to that of Mrs Hewitt's. Attitudes to the education of children were beginning to change. There was certainly a greater concern for their physical well-being, in part because the 1914-18 war had revealed the poor physique of the fighting forces. The Heads' logs now record

The Village School

*School Photograph – 1890.*
*Top row (left to right):* Albert Wildman, Frank Packwood, Reg Bateman, Tommy Ekins, Harry Garner, Percy Garner, John King, Sidney Farrar, Freddie Hewitt, Mrs Hewitt, Mr Hewitt, (headmaster).
*Second row:* Nellie Bass, Nellie Sharman, Lizzie Dennis, Lizzie Carrington, Alice Carrington, Mabel Mitchel, Lizzie Garner, Elsie King, Mabel King, Daisy Langley, Edith Langley, Elsie Hewitt.
*Front row:* Percy Wildman, Clara Bass, Florrie Sharman, Annie Denniss, Connie Valentine, Annie Valentine, Harry Mitchel, Bessie Valentine, Walter Valentine, Minnie King, Lily Langley.

63

*Miss Waldock's Class – 1926-27.*
*Back row (left to right): Gilbert Barker, George Cole, John Moss.*
*Middle row: Mr I'Anson (headmaster), Walter Smith, Phyllis Wise, Hubert Hancock, May Valentine, Henry Felce, Dorothy Wright, 'Cub' Westley, Nancy Hurn, Miss Waldock.*
*Front row: not known, Frances King, not known, Rootham, Sharman, Lilly Sharman, Harry Walker, not known, Horace Stevens, not known.*

The Village School

*Miss Waldock's Class – 1950-51.
Back row (left to right): Ruth Cambers, Anita Di Folco, Linda Watkins, not known, Dianne Berridge, Ruth Williams, Jennifer Salter, Miss Waldock, Catherine Stewart, Sonia Holyoak, Margaret Waldock, Diane Mynott.
Front row: Martin Packer, Roger Stringer, Michael Phillips, John Bollard, Gordon Ingle, David Bull, David Holyoak, not known, Richard Waller.*

frequent visits from doctors, nurses and dentists, but as comments by those who were there show, these weren't appreciated by the children!

Mr Albert Sharman, pupil from 1913 to 1922 didn't enjoy school. He remembers a Dickensian discipline – and some challenges to it!

*'Mr Hewitt had his desk on a raised platform with a window slightly open to one side. On one occasion he threatened to cane four of the boys for misconduct. He got hold of one and the other three ran for the open window. Two got out but the third one was "made sergeant". He received "three stripes" from the cane. He always carried his cane as he patrolled the classrooms. He would look over pupils' shoulders and if he wasn't satisfied with the work, a blow would be struck across the pupils' shoulders.*

*Occasionally the boys would knock a ball up onto the roof. (This was the sloping roof of the porch used as a cloakroom.) But they were not allowed to fetch it. If Mr Hewitt came out and caught the boys trying to retrieve their ball, they were in trouble. One boy nick-named Foxy stayed up on the roof from 10.30 am till 3.30 pm. He kept looking through the skylight window and the boys kept signalling to him when someone was coming. He missed his dinner he did. Next day, we all expected him to be caned for missing school but nothing happened.'* Mr Sharman believes that Mr Hewitt heard the boys saying they would sit on him if he did try to cane Foxy, and as this had happened once before, he decided not to go ahead. *'Some boys of 12 or 13 were quite large,'* he says.

The young Albert thought the teacher *'very unkind'* when he caned both hands of Nellie Porter from The Fox and Hounds, though they were covered with chilblains. He does confess to being naughty himself, along with five or six other boys. They did things like tie the girls' plaits together, and sometimes they got away with their misdeeds.

He remembers another occasion when the boys tried to burn Mr Hewitt's spare cane. They put it on the coal stove in the classroom. There were two coal stoves in what is now the hall. *'Unfortunately he saw it poking out of the stove and he held it flaming.'* This didn't cause a fire, but Mr Sharman does recall the fire of 1910, which destroyed the thatched roof. His brother Ron remembers the horses galloping by, pulling the Sharnbrook fire engine.

The young Albert was six when the 1914-1918 war began. He remembers writing in sand trays when young. As an older boy he mixed the ink in an enamel jug and filled china inkwells. During the war both boys and girls had to knit for the soldiers, but the girls were better knitters, he says. Mr Sharman thinks that 'Pip' Garner the teacher who taught knitting wasn't a very good knitter himself.

The main effect of the 1914-18 war, as far as the managers were concerned, was to put things *'on hold'*. School repairs and improvements had to wait. For the children it brought some welcome diversions. By 1916 there was a school garden and they grew produce for the war effort.

Mrs Driver, also at school during the First World War, remembers knitting socks and mittens for the soldiers. She lived in Dag Lane and was friends with Connie Sharman. Mrs Driver has happy memories, except for one incident. *'One day Mr Sharman's brother, Ron was in serious trouble. He had been playing truant and was called out in front of the class to the teacher's desk. Ron held out his hand ready to be caned, but at the last moment he pulled it away.'* Mrs Driver gasped in horror and the teacher caned Ron three times for pulling his hand away and Mrs Driver once for making a noise. Perhaps surprisingly, she remembers Mr Hewitt as *'strict but fair'*. Her favourite lessons were arithmetic and spelling. She also enjoyed the Friday afternoon nature walks and needlework. The girls' efforts at needlework were entered in the annual Flower Show and she won a prize for a nightdress. The other teacher she remembers is Miss King, the baker's daughter.

Mr Smith, a pupil from 1919 to 1928, particularly enjoyed sport and gardening. *'There were eight garden plots where the pool is now. On Friday afternoons the boys worked two to a plot. . . . At one time the girls were allowed to grow flowers on the borders between these plots of land. Sometimes the children showed the produce at the local Flower Show.'*

There does seem to be evidence of a more positive approach – more carrot and a little less stick perhaps? Some, particularly the boys who got caned more than the girls, might disagree with this view. The master's log for 1905 and 1908 records the delivery of medals and certificates for regular and perfect attendance. Mr Smith even recalls a more positive side of Mr Hewitt.

*'One day Mr Hewitt said there was a large weed on the communal plot and he would give 6d to the boy who could name it. This was a lot of money in those days. The boys stared and stared but could not see or name the huge weed. Finally Thomas Rootham pointed to it and named it as a rosebush. Mr Hewitt said a weed is any plant in the wrong place.'* And Thomas Rootham got the prize!

Mr Smith, who played for the school in both football and cricket teams, is one of the first former pupils to mention sport. *'The football pitch was behind the church at Maple Close and the posts and net were kept at the vicarage.'* He also remembers the new Practical Subjects Centre being opened in 1928, the year he left school. It is now the Nursery. It was for woodwork and cookery, including the preparation of school lunches for the children who now came from the villages of Yelden, Melchbourne, Pertenhall and Swineshead where the smaller village schools were closed. School dinners for local children didn't begin till 1942.

By this time Mr Hewitt had retired, and four heads had followed him, each staying only two years. Mr Smith, and many more Riseley residents remember the unusually named Mr I'Anson and his fine singing voice. *'He once sang on the wireless.'* Jack Hancock remembers his predecessor, Mr Clowes. *'He had a cupboard full of canes – all different thicknesses and according which punishment you had he selected one.'*

Mrs Gell, formerly Mary Rootham, has vivid memories of the school in the '20s when she was a pupil. Mr Clowes was Head from 1924 to 1926 and Mrs Gell is one of many who remembers his wife playing the piano for singing lessons. *'The older girls in the class used to think that she was wonderful because she wore such a lot of make up – nail polish, lipstick, rouge and powder.'*

Mrs Gell remembers getting on well with the teachers and thinking they were all lovely. They included Miss Waldock and Miss Chamberlain, later Mrs Bates. She says, *'The pupils had great respect for them even though they were so strict. They tended to dress in a very severe way – jumpers, thick stockings and skirts, which gave them the impression of being much older than they were. Some were probably only in their twenties.'*

Mrs Gell is right. Miss Waldock who lived with her parents at Town Farm and Miss Chamberlain who lived with her parents at the greenhouses on the Swineshead road, were in their twenties. Teachers tended to live locally as there was no transport. The bus came to Riseley only on Wednesdays and Saturdays.

Class lessons were very formal, Mrs Gell says. *'Desks faced the front and were fixed to the floor. You couldn't move without permission. There was no school uniform as such but the young girls wore white pinnies to school and the older girls wore gymslips. They all wore button-up boots. The boys wore hobnailed boots with "Blakeys" in them to make them last longer. Lessons included spelling, dictation, singing, cookery, sewing and gardening. All the work had to be completed carefully and properly with great pride. In the early school years the children practised their letters and numbers in sand trays. As they progressed up the school slates and then books were used. Once writing had been mastered in pencil, nib pens and ink were introduced. It was not unusual for the class to spend the whole morning learning how to form one letter properly. Multiplication tables were learned by chanting them.'*

There was great emphasis on doing things properly. Creativity and originality was not called for. Pupils were expected to form their letters, do their stitches, make pastry, or plant a row of beans *'properly'*. The cane was still used for girls as well as boys, and parents generally assumed that their children deserved the blows.

These reminiscences of school in the '20s and '30s show that the school retained many Victorian features. The Diocesan Inspector still called to test pupils on their knowledge of the Bible. The half-day holiday which followed his visit was greeted with excitement. Yearly exams were dreaded.

There was perhaps a bit more freedom in the school than in Victorian times. Mrs Gell remembers that on Friday afternoons after singing, children were permitted to play in Mr Valentine's field – where the car-park is now – during the last lesson of the day. There were Nature walks too and playtimes were fun with Catch, Hopscotch and – for the boys – Marbles. The yard did not have a hard surface and got muddy in winter but children played in the lane. They were not and had never been confined to school in the dinner hour. There were no school dinners for local children, who went home and played on the way.

Rounders, hoops and tops were popular. So was exploring the fields. Mrs Gell recalls an almost idyllic past. *'Nobody minded where their children went, and parents didn't have to worry about their children being in danger.'* In her memory only the regular visit of the dentist marred this happy time. She had to have teeth extracted on nearly every occasion. He performed the operation on the spot and the gums were only poorly numbed.

Mrs Neal, pupil from 1924 to 1933, also remembers the dentist as one of the worst things, but not the worst. She hated the school toilets. *'They were just a hole in the ground and were horrible!'* The master's log of 1931 echoes her opinion.

*'The school is conducted in bad conditions. The premises are on the Black list and the smell of the offices enters the school from the Girls' side and from the Boys' side if another prevails.'*

*'Offices'* is a euphemism. He is talking about those *'holes in the ground'*. These remained till 1934 when the pits were filled in and replaced by buckets *'as a temporary expedient to help fulfil the demands of the Board of Education'*. The buckets were still there in 1952 when Mr Williams writes: *' . . . there is no modern sanitation. The pails from the offices across the yard are emptied on a rubbish heap of many years standing, situated within a few yards of the Infants classroom and in close proximity to the road.'* They were there until the new block was built in 1962.

Back to Mrs Neal in the 1920s and '30s. On the whole she enjoyed school, especially netball and Christmas. *'There were concerts and the children went to the headteacher's house where his wife made them up for their different roles. There was a Christmas tree in the hall and all the children had presents from the tree.'*

Mrs Neal, grandchild of the baker in 69 High Street, remembers Miss Waldock teaching the *'babies'* and Miss Calthorpe who *'had coiled ringlets of hair like earphones'*. In the 1940-50s Mrs Neal's daughter went to the school. She remembers that in winter *'the school milk froze and the bottles were put by the fire in the big classroom which is now the hall to defrost'*.

Miss Benton started coming to Riseley school in 1923 when she was 11 and the school in Swineshead closed. She recalls three classrooms in what is now the hall, separated by curtains and heated by a large black coke stove. She also remembers *'the wonderful chocolate sponge cake'* made by Miss Parker the school cook. The wonderful aromas coming from the Cooking Centre made some of the Riseley children quite jealous of the bus children. She remembers Mr Holden, headteacher from 1928 to 1932 as *'very nice'*. He was her class teacher too and punished misdeeds by *'making you stand on a platform so that everyone could see you'*.

Miss Benton remembers being prevented from taking the 11 plus exam because she was asthmatic. Children passing this exam went to schools in Bedford or Kimbolton. Henry Waldock, Miss Waldock's younger brother, went to Kimbolton as a boarder. Kimbolton was for boys only and most day boys going to Kimbolton cycled there. Boys and girls going to Bedford cycled to Sharnbrook and caught the train. Teachers were very proud when they got children through the exam. Most children stayed at Riseley School till they were 14. This continued till 1962 when Margaret Beaufort School was built as a Secondary Modern School.

Mr Walker, a pupil from 1926 to 1935 recollects a big step forward into the 20th century – the installation of electric lights! This was paid for by an anonymous donor, thought to be the vicar. It happened in 1938, when Mr Walker had left school, but it made a big impression. Till this time all the lighting was by oil lamps or candles! There was no gas in the village. No wonder people remember the school as dark! And yet there were lectures and evening classes in the school from time to time.

The Second World War had a much bigger impact than the 1914-18 war, partly because of the evacuees. Miss Waldock, a teacher at the time, recalls sitting with the headmaster in September 1939 waiting for them to arrive. When they finally did they were unloaded upon the green, in front of The Five Bells and families chose which children they wanted.

Despite the large numbers, 94 evacuees to 60 Riseley children, it was decided not to start the double shift system operating elsewhere. Instead children from the outlying villages were sent back to be educated in their own villages and integration was attempted. This wasn't entirely successful.

Most of the children from St Joseph's RC school left with their teachers, but 12 stayed behind.

Mr Pope, pupil from 1935 to 1944 remembers the evacuees. *'They came from North London, from two schools St Joseph's RC School and Burleigh Central.'* The London children were probably appalled by the backwardness of our village. Mrs Ellen Di Folco certainly was, when she arrived with her family. She was horrified by lack of a proper toilet in her cottage and at the school.

Mr Pope says the older children, particularly the boys, enjoyed school life during the war. They were encouraged to do jobs in the village and could get time off from school to do them. The favourite was newspaper collecting which involved going round the village with a handcart. *'It was not unusual for the boys to tip the load so they could pick it up again or they might sit in the cottage reading the papers for most of the afternoons.'* At least they were reading!

Another popular activity was blackberrying and the subsequent jam making. In October 1941 this went on for a whole week, till a lorry from Shire Hall took the jam away. Pupils looked forward to doing this again in the following year, but the school received a telegram from Shire Hall saying their efforts weren't needed. Pupils did however make a further 53 pounds of jam!

Mr Pope remembers the school Christmas party in 1940. There was *'a tree from the Melchbourne estate, jellies made from gelatine and lemonade, no Christmas puddings because of rationing, classroom decorations made from painted waste paper glued into chains'*.

Miss Waldock remembers organising that party and others like it. She writes, *'During the years 1939-1945 when severe wartime restrictions and shortages were inflicted upon us, it was agreed that everything possible should be done to ensure that the children were not deprived of their simple pleasure, especially at Christmas time. The headmaster decided that the school party must take place as usual in spite of the added difficulties of providing for a large number of evacuees recently admitted to the school from danger zones in London and Kent.'*

She goes on to describe the fundraising efforts, which included a particularly successful Whist Drive in the Recreation Hall, and the preparations, which included a trip by all the teachers to buy a present for each child. *'With the children's letters to Santa Claus, written in class, as a guide to each one's wishes, we decided that the most appropriate place to begin our search would be Woolworth's Sixpenny Store, as it was known at the time.'* They had in fact 6d (2$^{1}/_{2}$p) for each infant, a shilling (5p) for each junior, and one shilling and sixpence (7$^{1}/_{2}$p) for the older children.

*'For 6d, our girls' presents included undressed baby dolls which we clothed before our party, tea sets, boxes of beads, skipping ropes, sewing and knitting sets, crayons, tracing and colouring books. For the boys various games eg Ludo, Snakes and Ladders, etc, Snap, Dominoes, toy cars, etc, drums, trumpets, mouth organs, jigsaw puzzles and a very good selection of various kinds of books, pencils and crayons.'*

Had anything like this happened in the 19th century? We cannot be sure. Perhaps there were kind teachers who made dolls clothes for their pupils, who paid attention to their wishes, but I think attitudes were changing. It was good for children to enjoy themselves! The newly arrived American servicemen certainly thought so. They too organised parties for the children – at Melchbourne and Thurleigh – and they threw sweets from their armoured vehicles as they drove through the village.

Not all evacuees came with official groups. Nor did they all go to Riseley Lower school. There was now an alternative, attracting people with some money to spare. John Ashworth, who wrote the foreword for this book, came to live with his grandfather, Mr Ashworth, the Air Raid Warden in Cherry Trees on the High Street when he was aged six.

He went to school at the vicarage, where the Reverend Paulson and his wife ran a preparatory school, coaching students for entry to Public schools. Deidhre Lube, another evacuee, went there and so after the war did David Howard, son of Jack Howard, a local farmer. Deidhre remembers classes of about eight - a great contrast with numbers at Riseley School and a reason why parents who could pay *'went private'*.

In 1957 there were 185 pupils in all and further room was needed. Class numbers were as follows:

| | | |
|---|---|---|
| Infants | 52 | Miss Waldock |
| Class 4 | 33 | Miss Childerley |
| Class 3 | 33 | Mrs Bull |
| Class 2 | 37 | Mrs Ashworth |
| Class 1 | 30 | Headmaster, Mr Williams |

Mr Williams, Head from 1940 to 1964, was a small Welsh man who aroused a variety of feelings. (There is an unexplained gap in the logs 1940 to 1952 so the views of Head and managers are unknown for this period.) Some villagers respected him as a disciplinarian and thespian. He put on great concerts in the Recreation Hall. Some remember him as sarcastic and as keen to cane and humiliate pupils as any of his predecessors. He was a traditionalist, but did preside over some important changes. The school became a primary school for pupils aged 5 to 11 in 1962 when Margaret Beaufort was built. It opened in 1962 and was named after Margaret Beaufort, mother of Henry VII founder of the Tudor dynasty, who was born at Bletsoe Castle in 1443.

In 1961 a new classroom block was built and the school had inside toilets at last!

But the next Head, Mr Calderbank, was critical of their siting and of other aspects of the new building. In December 1964 he regretted the *'traditional and orthodox plan of classrooms which lacked work bays, library corners, etc,'* and *'the lack of interest in the outside design of the new block: a mere rectangle, grey in colour. Lacks imagination in design. An opportunity for a really exciting experiment in school design has been lost.'*

The 1960s have arrived. A new word has appeared in the headmaster's log – imagination! Further changes followed. In 1965 the school got its first swimming pool.  Mr Sharman, former unhappy pupil, now chairman of the governors, opened the pool, the result of a great co-operative effort.  Parents worked hard to raise funds to match local authority grants.  Parental involvement was another innovative feature, though parents were first invited into school for a Parents Afternoon as early as 1936.  Classrooms looked very different now.  Mr Calderbank wrote:

*February 1967*   *Furniture to replace the unsuitable desks and chairs in Class 3 have arrived.  The headmaster would have preferred new trapezoidal types but understands costs will be saved if these reconditioned tables . . . are accepted.*

Mr Calderbank wanted trapezoidal tables so that pupils could sit in groups and discuss!  Children were being encouraged to talk!  Mr Calderbank gave the children their first school pet, a rabbit called Pierre Lapin!  Foreign languages too!  Pierre was in great demand for weighing and measuring tasks.  We are into learning through doing.  Pupils must understand.  It is a far cry from the rote learning and weekly tests of the 19th century that continued into the twentieth.  The 11 plus exam remained till 1969 when the comprehensive system was adopted.  Bedfordshire chose to organise this as three tiers – Lower, Middle and Upper schools.  Sharnbrook Upper School was built, taking village children out of the village to complete their education, for the first time.  Margaret Beaufort became a Middle School, taking pupils from nine to 13.  Riseley School became Riseley Lower School, taking them from five to nine.  In 1977 the Nursery was opened taking children from the age of three and four.

Changes since then have been so many that teachers are reeling.  In 1983 Riseley Lower School got its first female headteacher, Mrs Moyra Hobby.  Mrs Hobby prioritised re-equipping the school as in previous years the government allocation had not been spent.  Parents welcomed new books and equipment for maths, science and PE, but also found it hard to keep pace with change.  Some felt there was not sufficient formality or rigour as project work and free choice were introduced.  Testing became unfashionable.

Mrs Judy Ruff became Head in 1990 and started to prepare for the school's 150th anniversary. She invited ex-pupils into the school, trawled through the logbooks and wrote a history of the school which I have drawn on extensively to write this chapter.

In the 1990s tests reappeared as SATs. Special Attainment Targets have been introduced for children as young as seven. Children are tested when they start school, so that progress can be measured. The government has made priorities of literacy and numeracy. It wants to monitor progress and reward schools who bring it about! There is even talk about rewarding teachers who deliver the best results!

Looking back over more than 160 years, in some ways it does seem that the wheel has turned full circle, and we are back where we started. But it is also clear that a revolution has occurred. Riseley Lower School is no longer *'for the poor, labouring classes'*. It now serves a mixed but largely affluent area. It has to satisfy parents with high ambitions for their children. They want high standards in every way, materially, academically and spiritually. It is still a church school teaching Christianity, but most parents whether they attend church or not, are content with this. They want a school which educates the whole child. They believe that children learn when they are happy. They want a school that makes their children happy and successful! A revolution indeed!

# Farming in Riseley
**William Wallis**

Bedfordshire has long been an agricultural county, noted as a corn district. Until land drainage and mechanisation increased its potential, the northern tip of the county, with its heavy boulder clay, would not have been favourable land. Thomas Batchelor, a farmer and writer at the time of the Napoleonic Wars, described this land north of the Ouse as *'remarkable for cold wet clays and late harvests'*, the occupiers of which *'are said to be as poor as the soil'*.

Little is known of the early agricultural history of Riseley specifically. There is no evidence to suggest a settlement here before late Saxon times. The old English name meaning *'a clearing in the brushwood'* gives some indication of the nature of the land.

Mediaeval Riseley and the surrounding farmland would have been dominated by the manor, which was the economic and social unit of rural England. There are known to have been three manors in Riseley. It is possible that they existed before the Conquest, as large parts of the country were owned by *'thanes'* at the time of Edward the Confessor. Those who survived the coming of the Normans would have lost their free status under feudalism. Vacant or seized manors were widely distributed by William the Conqueror among his followers.

Under the manorial system in this area, the land was farmed on a two field rather than the more familiar three field system. The fields were cropped and fallowed in alternate years. In these two open fields bonded labourers, known as *'villeins'* or serfs, farmed scattered strips of land for their own subsistence as well as some for the support of the manor and its Lord. These strips were roughly an acre in size and were defined by the distance that the oxen could pull a plough without stopping: a furrow long or *'furlong'*. The ground would be turned to one side by the passage of the plough and on the return pass a ridge would be formed, giving rise to the distinctive *'ridge and furrow'* appearance. This has largely disappeared from Riseley since the extensive ploughing up of grassland during the First and Second World Wars, though it can still be seen in more pastoral parts of the county.

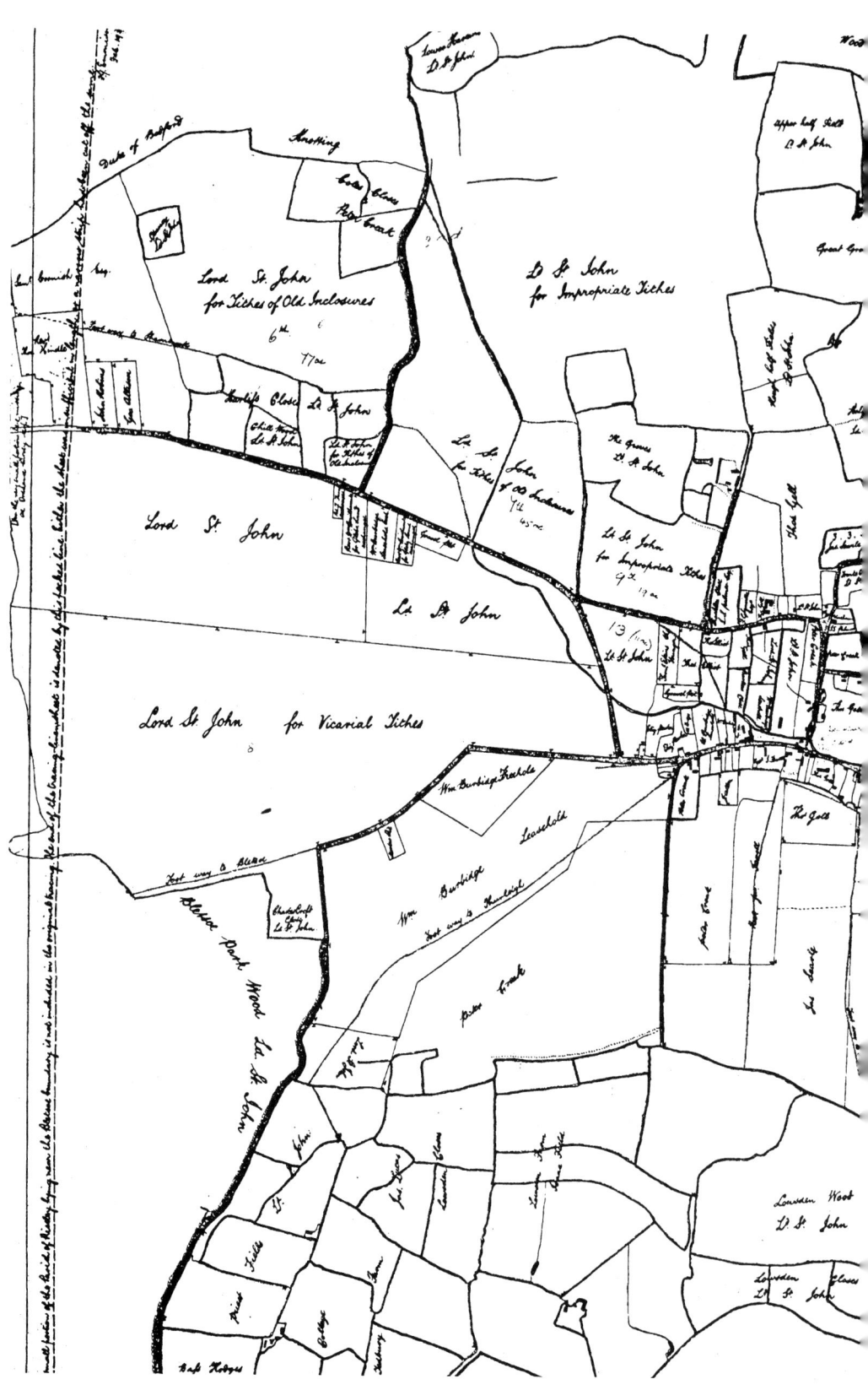

*Enclosure map*

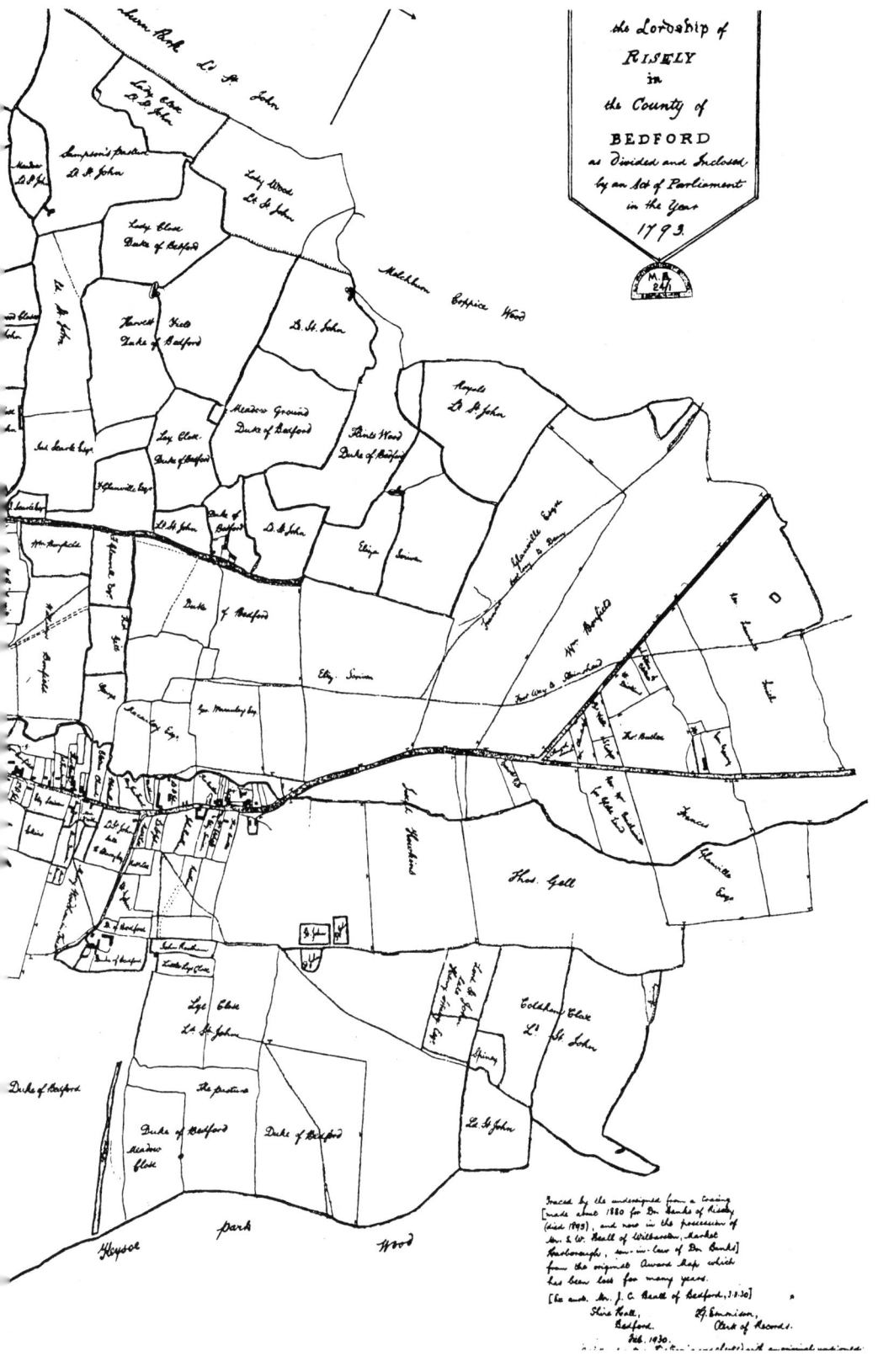

By the 15th century the bond between serf and lord had weakened due to a century of plague, famine, civil war and social unrest. The population decline and labour shortage allowed a new breed to rise – the yeoman farmer. Able men could now expand their holdings and many followed the example of the lords and enclosed land for their own use. While some thrived by buying or renting vacant land, others fell into great hardship and new inequalities arose within the village populations. Yeoman farmers were particularly prominent in this area of the county, perhaps because the land was hard to work, deterring those higher up the social scale and ensuring that only the strong and industrious from among the peasants would rise.

In 1792, Parliament passed the Enclosures Act in an attempt to rationalise agriculture, parish by parish. The Riseley Enclosure map was completed in 1793, indicating perhaps, that most of the changes had already taken place and only needed formalising. The act laid the foundations for the development of individual farms, resulting in the patchwork of cropped fields and the modern compact farmsteads of today.

A glance at the Riseley Enclosure map provides an invaluable insight into the state of agriculture at the end of the 18th century. The rise of the yeoman farmer is illustrated by the considerable number of properties bearing the name of Thomas Gell or William Bonfield. Smaller holdings also abound and it is interesting to identify the cottages and to see that many of the old field boundaries are recognisable today, although inevitably, some amalgamation has occurred due to increased mechanisation. Also of note, is a windmill to the north-east of the village towards Swineshead. Although some land is owned or held by the Church, the dominant landowners are the Duke of Bedford and Lord St John.

The St John family, who had owned extensive estates in North Bedfordshire since the time of the Norman Conquest, added Bletsoe Castle and its lands in the 15th century through marriage to Margaret Beauchamp, mother of Margaret Beaufort. In the early 1600s they acquired Melchbourne Park from the Duke of Bedford, to whom it had been given by Queen Elizabeth I. Soon after the Enclosure map was drawn up, the Duke of Bedford chose to consolidate his estates to the south of Bedford, around Woburn Abbey and sold his remaining lands in Riseley to Lord St John. Thus, by the mid-19th century, most of the land in Riseley was owned by the Melchbourne Estate.

This was the golden era of the great estates, when prominent landowners, such as the Duke of Bedford at Woburn, led the way in the application of new scientific methods of animal and plant husbandry. It was a time of invention and investment. Agriculture became more mechanised and steam power was introduced. The independent yeoman had largely disappeared and workers took a pride in belonging to their estate, enjoying a prolonged period of stability.

However, by the end of the century, agriculture was in the grip of a deep depression. This resulted in greatly reduced rental income from the tenanted land and in the early 1900s with several quick deaths in the St John family and the ensuing demand for death duties, the financial pressure increased to the point where the sale of parts of the estate became unavoidable. This marked the beginning of the end for the Melchbourne Estate. The constituent farms were sold off and some have changed hands several times since the 1930s when this process began. Unusually, most of them are still family farms, as opposed to parts of large farm companies. Whether they will remain so, as farming enters the next period of depression, is yet to be seen.

The following history of Riseley farms is predominantly derived from the taped recollections of those involved in farming in Riseley over their lifetime. Consequently, the time it spans is mainly within living memory. However, this period has surely seen some of the most significant and rapid changes in farming life and practice of the last millennium.

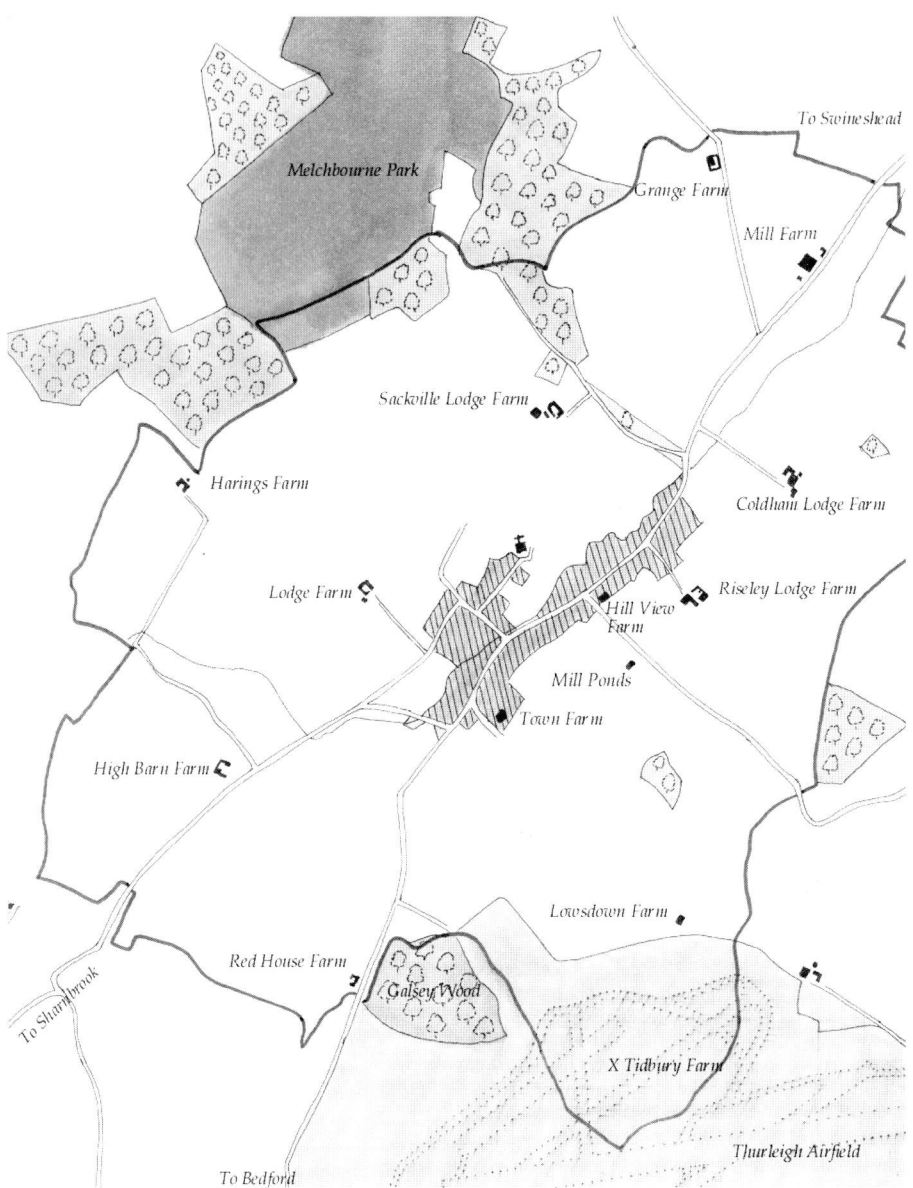

*Map of the parish of Riseley showing the farms*

**High Barn Farm** is situated to the Southwest of Riseley, about half a mile from the village by the side of the Sharnbrook road. The land was part of the St John estate and was recorded so on the Enclosure map, though no buildings are shown. The farmstead had been built by the time of the 1862 estate map and the tenant was William Whitehead. He was also renting High Barn House on Riseley High Street which was originally the farmhouse to High Barn, but this has not been so within living memory. The house at the farm was designed as two farm workers' cottages, with the brick buildings behind forming animal sheds and stockyard.

*High Barn Farm*

One of the members of the Rootham family (probably Daniel, father of Bani), came to High Barn after William Whitehead. He is known to have been a farmer as well as a tenant miller at the windmill on Mill Hill (Keysoe Road). It is said that there was a line of sight between the farm and the windmill and that messages were signalled between the two at meal times.

Bill Brown farmed at High Barn following the Roothams and is remembered by older residents. Ralph Savage took over the tenancy in 1930 and his son Aubrey and his family moved to High Barn to run the farm.

*Ralph Savage with his binder*

The contracting firm of Savage was also run by the family, using steam threshing and cultivating machinery. It had been founded in 1849 by Ralph's father Charles, a yeoman farmer from Bourne End, Bletsoe, and was based at Mill Lane, Riseley where the engine sheds and workshop were situated. Ralph oversaw the business from 71 High Street, as well as being a long-serving collector of rates and taxes; his other two sons, Eustace and Roland, ran the contracting. He was a progressive farmer in his day, being the first in Riseley to own a binder, which bound the cut corn to make a sheaf, an advance on the earlier reaper which only cut the corn. He also owned a motor car!

The firm carried out much estate work for Lord St John, the Duke of Bedford and the Marquess of Northampton, as well as carrying out contracts for many other farmers. They also moved timber from all around the county. Many of the farms in Riseley used Savages for either threshing or cultivating. The first set of steam ploughing tackle had been bought in 1875, but by far the busiest period was during the Second World War, when there was tremendous pressure to plough out grassland for cropping.

The work rate of a steam plough would compare well to a modern tractor and plough combination but was a lot more complicated to carry out: two steam engines were required, one on either side of the field to be ploughed. These pulled a reversible plough between them using steel cables on revolving drums under the engines. The plough was on wheels, had four to six furrows and was steered by a man who rode on it. The men working the engines signalled using steam whistles and were supplied with coal and water by the farmer. (A system had been devised using pulleys and an anchor, whereby one steam engine could pull the plough, but this was not used by Savages.) Cultivating, subsoiling and moledraining were carried out in much the same way.

*Engine and timber dolly, Tavistock Street, Bedford – Jake Clarke and Aubrey Savage*

The threshing contracts were worked differently and the individual farmers hired a steam engine (with a driver), a threshing drum (with an operator) and a straw-elevator or chaff cutter, as required. The farm workers and helpers would then be used to make up the threshing gang: two or three would be needed on the stack of corn sheaves to keep the drum operator supplied. His job was to cut the binding on the sheaves and feed them into the top of the drum, which was a large machine on wheels, driven by a belt and pulley from the steam engine. It carried out the same job as the internal workings of a modern day combine harvester – it separated the grain from the straw. The grain was bagged off and one man worked on the sack outlets. Another man collected the chaff (small straw and dust) while two more men handled the loose threshed straw from the elevator, building it into stacks for winter use. Alternatively, the straw could be put through a chaff cutter and used for feed. In time, a baler was designed to work with the threshing drum.

The entire threshing gang, therefore, involved eight or nine men with another needed to keep the steam engine supplied with coal and water – a huge labour requirement! Savages employed many local men with their contracting, including Frank Porter, Len Neal, Charlie Gell, Dick and Jack Sawford, Len Register, Les Stringer, George Smith, Walt Smith and Eric Hancock.

*Engine and threshing drum, circa 1905*

Aubrey used the engines at High Barn for cultivating and threshing, though the farm had its own small steam engine for running the animal feed mill. It also had its own labour force - Joe Smith, Fred Gell and John Brown. The farm itself was typical of the small mixed farms before the Second World War, running cattle, sheep and pigs and growing most of the animal feed. Horses were still used extensively at this time and Aubrey's children Una, Beryl and Pat remember them very well, in particular a blind horse called '*Captain*' who would rest his muzzle on the back of '*Kit*', another horse, to be led into the stable. They also remember an especially friendly pig that could open the yard gate and would regularly visit them in the cottages!

During the Second World War, many changes occurred: the push to plough up grassland was immense and resulted in the disappearance of much livestock, while many hedges were removed and the smaller, individual fields started to amalgamate. High Barn was in the middle of a huge American airforce bomb dump, which stretched from the *'Toll-bar'* (by the Sharnbrook turn) at Riseley to the A6 at Sharnbrook, with stacks of bombs (without detonators!) on the sides of the Sharnbrook road. Una and Beryl remember that a special pass was needed for everyone at the farm even to get to school, but that later Italian and German prisoners of war worked at the farm and some were allowed to bike back to their camp unescorted! Food rationing was in operation, but was not felt as badly on the farms and at High Barn there were always US servicemen around who would bring tinned peaches, oranges, sweets and cigarettes to exchange for *'cackle-berries'* (eggs). There was plenty of game to be shot too, as the estate gamekeepers could not operate on the farm because of the bombs!

Farm machinery was also changing, with tractors becoming more common and popular. Farmers were using the steam engines less and even though Savages changed over to Field Marshall tractors the contracting business was in terminal decline. However, a new use was found for the old ploughing engines, which steam sterilised the soil in glasshouses. The threshing side disappeared with the introduction of combine harvesters, and with the death of Ralph in between the premature deaths of Eustace and Roland, the firm of Savage ceased operating a short time after celebrating its centenary. The machinery was sold and many of the steam engines were scrapped. Some, however, were sold on and have been seen in recent years at working demonstrations.

Ralph's death had major consequences for Aubrey at High Barn, which had been bought in the early 1950s by T A Saul when the last of the St John farms was sold. The tenancy was in Ralph's name and Aubrey was forced to leave the farm as there was then no security of tenure. He and his family moved into 71 High Street, Riseley, where the farming connection was continued by Aubrey running a smallholding, Una marrying Tony Shelton whose family farmed at Pertenhall and Beryl marrying Charles Wallis at Lodge Farm.

After T A Saul sold High Barn it was acquired by the Church Commissioners who also owned neighbouring Harings Farm. The tenancy was taken on by the Clifton family, who farmed Harings. The two farms are still run together today.

**Harings Farm** is situated to the north-west of Riseley, on the edge of the parish, almost a mile away from the village and is accessed by a farm road leading on from Knotting Lane, which joins the Sharnbrook road next to High Barn Farm.

The square brick-built farmhouse is typical of the old estate farms and the farm has retained some of the traditional stockyard and outbuildings behind it. Modern farm buildings and two cottages have been added in later years.

The 1793 Enclosure map does not show any farmstead; the land was owned by Lord St John and two of the fields were known as *'Upper and Lower Hareins'*. The tenant shown on the 1862 St John estate map was Joseph Nicholls. In more recent years, the farm had a succession of tenants: Mr Larkinson, followed by Edward Horrell in 1923. He was paying a rent of 13s 6d (67$^{1}$/$_{2}$p) per acre - this had risen to £4/acre in the 1950s. An equivalent modern rent would be about £50/acre. In 1927, the farm was sold privately by Lord St John to Alfred and Sarah Louise Backhouse, and the last tenants before the Second World War were Messrs Measures and Forgham.

The farm was taken on by the Ministry of Agriculture (the *'War Ag'*) at the outbreak of the War. This was a common practice with derelict or inefficient farms, with the push to maximise production. They ploughed out most of the grass to grow cereals and even used the empty farmhouse to store bagged grain. By the late 1940s the War Ag was winding down and the farm was again let, on two year tenancies in 1949 to Mr Davies, followed by Mr Lammy in 1951. Fred Clifton took over the tenancy in 1953, became a full tenant after the initial two years and his son Ian and his family still live and farm at Harings.

In 1956 the Ministry of Agriculture sold the farm to the Church Commissioners, who subsequently acquired neighbouring High Barn Farm when it was sold by T A Saul. The two farms have since been farmed together.

Farming in Riseley

The Cliftons came from a mixed farm near St Neots and they re-stocked Harings Farm with beef cattle and pigs. The latter were kept in the old buildings with some running outside in the summer. The cattle required a lot of grass and this was rented away from the farm wherever it was available. Some was re-seeded on the farm as a break crop along with alfalfa, beans, brussels, potatoes and cereals. The last cattle left the farm in the early 1990s.

Although a workhorse was brought to the farm – Ian remembers hoeing brussels with it – Harings was mechanised. A combine was used with grain being stored in sacks initially and later in silos and on floor in bulk. Fred Clifton had one of the first combines at their previous farm, a petrol-engined John Deere from America, which had been allocated during the War by drawing names from a hat due to the shortage of machines!

*Hoeing brussels – Lily Felce at Riseley Lodge Farm*

Crawlers were used in preference to tractors and the farm did all its own cultivation and ploughing. The animal manure was spread by machine, although Ian remembers this job being done with a horse at St Neots. Soot was used as a basic fertiliser and this was spread by hand – a very dirty job!

*Crawler tractor at Grange Farm*

The straw from the cereal crops was predominantly baled for the stock, though any excess was burnt in the field; during the War, this could only be done during daylight hours because of the blackout.

In the 1960s, the farm employed up to 20 men including George Smith and Harry Walker from Riseley, with the high labour requirement of the stock, brussels and potatoes. This gradually reduced with changes in cropping and farming practice, and now Harings and High Barn are run by Steven and Michael Prowse, Ian's stepsons.

In the late 1970s, Ian started to diversify into agricultural contracting, mainly cultivation and muck spreading. This contracting business is still operating, now run by Michael and Stephen in addition to the farm. A new venture called Sporting Targets was constructed in recent years on a new site at the end of Knotting Lane. Initially a clay pigeon shoot, it has developed many additional rural and leisure activities, which are co-ordinated by Ian and his son Andrew.

**Lodge Farm** is located to the west of Riseley and is reached from a farm road leading off Rotten Row, though the original farm entrance was at the junction of The Butts and Sharnbrook road.

The farmhouse is unusual, being three storeys high at the front but only two at the back, with an asymmetrical roof. The back of the house is older and was possibly farm cottages which were renovated when the front section was completed in early 1810. It is joined on to the brick farm buildings behind, which form the traditional stockyard. Modern buildings and corn storage silos have been erected more recently around the farmyard.

*Stock yard at Lodge Farm*

The old buildings are similar to those on many of the old estate farms in design and layout, which were probably all built over the same period. Dates stamped into the bricks at Lodge Farm are from 1852 and 1875, which was the period when many of the big estates were at their peak. This also coincided with the ending of the Brick Tax in 1850, encouraging good landlords to improve tenant farmhouses and buildings. They also began to improve the farmland, with clay piped underdrainage being installed to allow the full potential of the cold, wet clay soils of North Bedfordshire to be exploited.

Alongside the date stamps at Lodge Farm are the initials J E W, which undoubtedly belong to John Williamson, a builder living in Riseley at the turn of the 19th century. His son Sam, who carried on the building business, is remembered by many in the village.

The farm was part of the St John estate and was marked as such on Enclosure. The estate map of 1862 records the tenants as John and Thomas Woodruffe, but the farm is called *'The Grange'* with the farm now known as Riseley Grange being referred to as *'Sandhill'*.

John Hartop was tenant in the late 1800s and married Frances Waldock, whose brother David farmed at Town Farm. When he left the farm in 1915, the tenancy was taken on by Sid Williams and his brother Montague. Mont subsequently married a daughter of Sam Westley (who farmed at Sackville Lodge) and moved to their farm at Cleat Hill near Bedford.

In 1932, Lodge Farm became the first of the St John estate farms to be sold and Sid Williams, with no security of tenure and having received twelve months notice, had to leave. The farm was bought by Charles Gardner, who soon after also acquired the farms of Sackville Lodge, Eastfields and Melchbourne Grange. Charles himself farmed at Pulloxhill, so he brought his brother-in-law, Fred Wallis and his family to Lodge Farm. Fred's older son Harold later became manager for the other farms.

Charles Gardner's approach to agriculture was quite revolutionary and he proceeded to plough up the old grassland, with the help of the local contractors – the Savages and their steam engines. He reseeded with wild white clover, a legume, which improved the fertility of the soil by absorbing nutrients from the air. This, coupled with deep soil busting, moledraining and the control of rabbits, allowed Charles to succeed when many farmers in the depression years of the 1930s, were finding it hard to make a living. Many of the techniques he advocated were later adopted during the Second World War, when much grassland was ploughed. He became an Alderman and Chairman of the Agricultural and Smallholding Committee of Bedfordshire County Council, on which he served for 30 years, as well as serving on the

Magistrates' Bench. A plaque was erected and a row of trees was planted in recognition of his services during the Festival of Britain in 1951 and can still be seen by the side of the Swineshead road, to the north of Riseley.

At Lodge Farm, the Wallis family initially ran the farm for Charles Gardner. They then became tenants in their own right, until his death in the early 1960s when Harold and his younger brother Charles bought the farm. It was later divided between them and they and their sons still farm their own units at Lodge Farm.

In the 1930s, it was a mixed farm with free range hens, pigs, sheep and beef cattle being kept. At this time, the stock was still moved on foot and Harold remembers collecting a herd of 42 bullocks from the far side of Bedford and walking them right through the town and back to Riseley. On another occasion, Fred and Charles collected a herd of pedigree Hereford heifers and a bull from Sharnbrook railway station at dusk; they had walked them as far as the A6 road on the way home, when the cattle bolted into the darkness and disappeared! They were found in the morning behind Pippin Wood.

The farmland was mainly down to grass, which was gradually reseeded with wild white clover; this was grazed and in a good year cut for a valuable crop of seed. Wheat was grown on the arable land but did not yield well - $1^1/_2$ tonnes per acre being a good crop. Nowadays, with modern varieties, fertilisers and agro-chemicals, coupled with improved management techniques, a crop yielding 3 tonnes per acre is average, while yields in excess of 4 tonnes per acre are not unusual.

Most of the grass was ploughed out during the Second World War when Enforcement Orders were issued by the Ministry of Agriculture, with the resulting loss of livestock and increase in crops. Charles remembers some of the rougher grazing land needing bushes and shrubs pulling out before ploughing. Savages had been used for threshing (as well as ploughing), but during the War a Massey Harris combine was bought in crates and built on the farm; it was the first combine in the village and had its own engine to work the mechanism, but needed pulling. A self-propelled International model was bought later. These were both bagger combines and a bag drier was installed in one of the buildings to handle wet grain; this was used as late as 1977 (a very wet harvest)!

*Massey-Harris bagger-combiner at Lodge Farm*

Tractors were also appearing, with the first new Standard Fordson costing £175 on iron wheels. During the War, new machinery could not be bought on rubber tyres due to the shortage of rubber following the Japanese invasion of the Far East and priority was given to military vehicles. Car tyres could be obtained with a special permit, but only replacements for farm machinery.

Much of the straw was baled for home use or sale and both Harold and Charles remember the early Allis Chalmers round baler as being a very good machine and well before its time. One year, all of the straw was sent to a paper mill in Kent. The grain was sold through the Corn Exchange in Bedford on a Saturday afternoon, when a sample was taken in from the farm and the merchants would value it on appearance. Modern merchants use laboratory analysis to evaluate grain today and deduct from the price or reject loads of grain for minute differences in any one out of five or six quality criteria. In the early days Hipwells, the millers at Sharnbrook, bought most of the local grain.

The farm workforce has changed over the years. When the Wallis family took over from Sid Williams, his men stayed on and included Ken Rootham (Bani's son), Ken Spavins and John Brown (uncle to Tony Cerasale who later worked at Town Farm). At busy times, extra help could be obtained from the local men who worked on the other farms managed by Harold. During the War, German prisoners of war were used with one actually living in one of the farm buildings. Evacuees were billeted in the farmhouse. On one occasion, an army regiment from a nearby camp brought its men and lorries to help gather the harvest.

Nowadays, Harold's younger two sons, David and Richard, run their farm with one workman, John Gratton, who has been at Lodge Farm for nearly 35 years. Charles' son William runs their side of the farm, with seasonal help at harvest. Both Charles and Harold maintain an active interest in farming at Lodge Farm.

**Sackville Lodge Farm** is situated at the north-western end of the village, off the old Carriage Drive roadway to Melchbourne Park.

The existing brick buildings originally consisted of a traditional stockyard surrounded by loose boxes and animal sheds, with the farmhouse on one side; the rickyard (where the sheaves of corn were built into ricks for winter threshing) was quite unusual, being enclosed by a brick wall.

Some of the old buildings remain today, alongside more modern agricultural buildings that have been added more recently. The old farmhouse is now privately owned.

The Enclosure map of 1793 shows the farm belonging to The Duke of Bedford. However, by the time the St John estate map was drawn up in 1862 it was included in that estate, the tenant being Joseph Eaton. Sam Westley was the last estate tenant to farm the land and left when the farm was sold in the 1930s, setting up a livery stable business in the village. His great grand-daughter and her husband, Barbara and Cliff Middleton, still run the livery stables in Riseley.

*Rickyard with thatched ricks*

The farm was bought by Dick Sedgewick who farmed it for several years before selling to his brother-in-law, Charles Gardner.

In 1942, the farm was sold again, to Jack Wilkinson whose family still lives and farms at Sackville. On buying the farm Jack was advised by the auctioneers to move in rapidly as the US Army was looking to requisition the farmhouse for billets. They were already in Melchbourne Park House and storing bombs in woods round the farm. He and his family moved in the next day!

The farm was a traditional mixed farm up to the Second World War, with crops being grown to feed the farm stock and any surplus being sold. The War resulted in a large loss of grassland with the drive to grow more corn.

Jack was a nurseryman; his family had owned a nursery at Willington before he bought Sackville Lodge but he approached arable farming with enthusiasm. He planted and successfully grew cabbages, potatoes, brussels and cereals, with cattle, sheep and pigs running on the remaining grass. In the first season, 90 acres of cabbages were grown (a huge area) with the help of land army girls and German prisoners of war. Twelve POWs were still billeted in the farm cottages until they were repatriated after the end of the war.

*Charles Gardner's dispersal sale at Sackville*

Mechanisation was accelerating at this time, though steam engines were used in the beginning for cultivating and threshing the corn. One of the drawbacks of steam was the problem of sparks produced by the engines and this resulted in a serious fire in the rickyard one year, in which a threshing drum and several corn and straw stacks were lost. The farm buildings were only saved by the timely intervention of the US firemen from Melchbourne Park, galvanised into action by the close proximity of thousands of bombs!

Tractors came to Sackville Lodge quite early and it was the first farm locally to import a row crop tractor – an Allis Chalmers B on iron wheels – to work in the vegetable crops. It was also the first to use a specialised mechanical planter.

With the marriage of his elder son Peter to Jean in 1951, Jack was able to sell him the arable land and to concentrate on the fledgling nursery he was building.

Jean well remembers her first harvest at the farm in 1952, which was extremely wet. The corn was harvested by a towed Allis Chalmers bagger combine and the bags were so wet they would not dry naturally and had to be taken off-farm to a bag dryer in Knotting. The addition to the farm buildings of bulk grain storage bins which allowed hot air to be blown through to dry the grain, was the result.

*Jack Wilkinson working on the cabbage planter*

The pig unit was expanding quickly from an initial herd of seven sows to a peak of nearly a 1000, producing 200 weaners a week, initially to sell and then later to fatten. To begin with they were all outdoors, which was not ideal because of the heavy clay soil, so the pig buildings were built. These had insulated floors for the piglets, made up of buried glass bottles, collected by the local dustmen. Much of the barley produced on the farm was milled for the pig rations and most of the cereal straw used for bedding.

However, pig economics have always been volatile and numbers were gradually cut back until production was stopped in the 1980s – first the breeding sows and finally the fattening unit – leaving the piggery redundant.

The cattle were also gone, most of the cows being sold in the 1950s and then later the calves which were for a time bucket-reared and fattened in the farmyard.

A flock of sheep grazes the remaining grassland, which is used as a runway by Peter and Jean's eldest son, Tim, to operate a flying club. The runway has been in existence (in various locations, depending on the grassland rotation) since 1946 when Jack bought his first aeroplane, an ex-RAF trainer, and built the hangar.

The arable farm is run by the youngest son, Ike, with seasonal help at harvest time, in stark contrast to the early years, when seven men were employed in the piggery plus five more on the vegetables.

**Sackville Nursery** was started by Jack Wilkinson at the end of the Second World War with second-hand glasshouses bought from the Lea Valley near London. It continued to expand and passed to his younger son, David, on Jack's death. When the unit was at its peak, it had over two acres under glass and employed some 15 people, mainly women. Tomatoes were grown initially, when the demand was for food, with later production switching to flowers. Carnations were grown very successfully until the 1970s, when advances in transport and handling resulted in a flood of imports from South Africa, Kenya and Columbia causing the home market to crash. The carnations were, therefore, replaced by chrysanthemums.

Chrysanthemums required a more complicated growing regime, with the need to manage the amount of light and dark they received in order to produce flowers. This was achieved by the use of artificial lights in the winter and blackout shades in the summer. The shades also acted as insulation when used after dark in the winter.

Irrigation with liquid feed replaced the old methods of animal manure and solid artificial fertiliser, as it was more precise.

Control of diseases was chiefly carried out by the steam sterilisation of the beds prior to planting a crop. Pests became an increasing problem, requiring more and more chemical control with the arrival of imported species.

The glasshouses were heated using boilers originally run on coal. Full automation was achieved with the introduction of oil firing.

The flowers grown were packaged and sent to the large markets in London, Birmingham and Manchester, plus smaller markets in Sheffield and Leicester, by rail from Sharnbrook Station. However, as this became more expensive, local road hauliers were used.

A combination of factors in the 1990s, including delivery problems, greatly increasing costs of oil and electricity and falling demand and prices due once again to imported flowers, led to the nursery ceasing production in 1999 when David retired.

**Mill Farm Nursery** is situated to the north-east of Riseley along the Swineshead road. At the time of the Enclosure survey of 1793 the farm belonged to an E Geary and included a corn windmill. The windmill was still present on later maps, but within living memory all that survived were the base and foundations.

The land around the farm in 1793 was in the names of various individuals, including a large enclosure to the east in the name of the Revd Lawrence Smith. The 1862 map for the St John estate records the farm being owned by the vicar of Warden, continuing the ecclesiastical connection. However, in the early 1900s the land was bought by the Chamberlain family, who ran a smallholding there with cattle and pigs for many years. Their daughter was a teacher at the village school.

The nursery is a relatively recent addition to the farm. In 1938 the Chamberlains sold the farm to the Vincents, who ran a nursery in Wormley, Hertfordshire and Les, his wife and sons Gordon and Brian moved in.

At this time, there were no nurseries in north Bedfordshire because of the cold, heavy clay soil; most were situated on the easier soils to the south and east of Bedford, around Willington, with the added advantage of easier and quicker access to the London market, via the Great North Road – the A1.

The glasshouses were erected in 1938 by Duncan and Tucker, nursery builders from the Lea Valley (a large glasshouse area). They were paid for after one year when the first crop was harvested. The initial area of glass was $3/4$ acre, but this was extended in 1949-50 to $1\,1/4$ acres, comprising eight glasshouses, 150' long by 25' wide, all timber-framed.

The remaining land was under grass and was ploughed up during the War. Les Vincent had no machinery of his own because of the size of the smallholding, so this work was carried out by the War Ag and charged to the farm. Once ploughed, the land was cropped with cereals. Savages were used for threshing. When the War Ag finished in the 1950s, the land was once again sown down to grass and sheep were kept.

In the glasshouses, cucumbers were grown for a short time until War broke out in 1939, when they were banned by the Ministry of Agriculture, because they were not considered to be a wholesome food. Production was changed completely to tomatoes, which were considered good for the diet in the absence of imported fruit. This was regulated by the Ministry which controlled the selling price from producers right through the retailers and the selling outlets. Les Vincent could only sell to two greengrocers – Mayes in Kimbolton and Hills in Rushden. This was to try to prevent the emergence of a black market. In addition to the ripe tomatoes, tomato plants were produced to enable people to grow their own in gardens and allotments – *'Dig for Victory'*! After the war, cucumbers were grown once again, accounting for some 50% of the nursery area.

Inside the glasshouses, the crops were grown on raised beds made up of alternate layers of horse manure, soil and straw. Huge quantities of manure were required and were sourced locally from Wesley's stables and also from further afield – wagons would be delivered to Sharnbrook Station from the Horse Guards' stables in London. This mix had to be dug over by hand to form the beds. Additional fertilizer was applied using a blood, fish and bone compound and also dried seaweed.

Before new crops could be planted, the soil needed to be sterilised to kill any harmful pests and diseases. With cucumbers, the only way to do this was by steaming carried out by digging pipes some 18" under the beds and blowing the steam from a hired steam engine into the soil. This was a very laborious, time-consuming task and was later replaced by sheet steaming, whereby a cover was sealed over the bed and steam pumped under this and left to settle into the soil.

*Les Vincent in the cucumber house*

The tomato beds were sterilised by soaking them in liquid formaldehyde.

The crops had an annual season with the seeds being set in the propagating house around the end of December and then planted out into the beds in late February. Cucumbers could be cut from the end of March to October, and tomatoes picked from early May to October.

Throughout the season, the crops were very dependent on temperature and humidity. Heat was required throughout the colder months and was supplied by boilers running 24 hours a day, seven days a week. These were originally hand-stoked with coal (delivered to Sharnbrook Station), which was later replaced by a self-feed system and eventually oil-firing. The water heated in the boilers circulated on a gravity system (the glasshouses were built on a rising slope and hot water rises). The hot water pipes used were salvaged from the Crystal Palace in London after it was destroyed by fire.

Humidity and ventilation were controlled by the opening of roof vents and windows. Water for irrigation was supplied from a land drain filled reservoir, from where it was pumped to a water tower and gravity fed to the glasshouses. To begin with, the crops were watered by hand with a hose; later on a rubber piped drip irrigation system was installed, which could also be used to deliver liquid feed.

The labour requirement for tomatoes and cucumbers was large, all jobs being done manually from bed preparation, the plant trimming through the summer to the picking, grading and packaging. During the War, German and Italian prisoners of war were sent to help, with land army girls providing extra casual labour at peak times. After the war, five full-time staff were employed plus family labour and seasonal help for summer packing.

In the early days (apart from the War years), all the produce was sent by train from Sharnbrook Station to Covent Garden market in London. Later on, road haulage was used to supply Leicester market.

Unfortunately, from the 1970s onwards, the economics of glasshouse vegetable production changed. Fuel prices soared with the oil crisis, cheap imports from abroad were becoming more plentiful and home demand and prices were static. Despite changing to *'cold crops'*, whereby less heating was required, the end was inevitable and the nursery stopped production in 1994.

**Grange Farm** is to the north of Riseley, a mile from the village, next to the Dean road. The farmhouse and the old buildings are built in the traditional brick style, with modern farm buildings adjacent to them. The farm cottages are situated to the north of the farmyard, on the opposite side of the road.

There is no farmstead marked on the Enclosure map and the land shown nearest to Riseley was farmed by William Bonfield and Francis Glanville. The St John estate map of 1862 shows the tenant to be John Smith; the farmstead was built by this time, though the farm was named *'Sandhill'*, which was possibly an estate title or nickname due to the light, sandy soil that occurs around the farm.

John William Love was tenant at the turn of the 19th century and was followed by the Conquest family, who are remembered by people in the village. They lived in the farm cottages. The farmhouse had been moved into in the early 1900s by Henry St John after his household became too small for Melchbourne Park. After the St John family left The Grange, the house was let to the two Miss Gearish's, who ran it as a guest house. It was very popular with London families for holidays and offered croquet, tennis and pony riding.

*Grange Farm House*

During the 1930s, a very well attended Point-to-Point meeting was held at The Grange. This was further enhanced by the participation of the Prince of Wales, who was soon to be Edward VIII.

The Conquests left Riseley Grange in the 1950s, when the farm was bought by T A Saul, who also purchased Coldham Lodge in Riseley and Eastfields and Melchbourne Grange Farms in neighbouring parishes. A farm manager, Johnny Merriken was appointed and lived in The Grange farmhouse, with the farm office in one of the outbuildings.

T A Saul already farmed in the flatlands of Lincolnshire and he introduced many changes to his farms in Bedfordshire. A variety of new crops were grown: asparagus, artichokes, French beans, cauliflowers, onions, sweetcorn and even mushrooms in the old farm buildings. These were in addition to the more usual crops of wheat, barley, peas, beans and grass for seed; large areas of brussels sprouts were also grown and are thought to be the cause of the flocks of wood pigeons now common in the area.

Larger machinery was used and many hedges were removed to accommodate it within bigger fields. Much of the ploughing and cultivating was carried out by Northerns and their crawler tractors from Harrold.

The removal of hedges was quite common on a number of farms at this time, due in part to the increasing size of the machinery and also to the move away from animals needing field boundaries to fence them in. The reduction in full-time agricultural labour resulted in far fewer men being available in winter months for maintaining the existing hedges and ditches. This was partially offset by the development of mechanical hedge trimmers and diggers for the ditches. In more recent years, many new hedges and trees have been planted.

With the arrival of a new farm manager, Jim Turnbull (who was based in Melchbourne), Rosemary Nuttal and her husband, who both worked for T A Saul, came to live at The Grange farmhouse. Rosemary remembers the large acreages of potatoes and brussels destined for markets in Swansea, Brighton and Smithfield in London, being picked by hand before machines were widely used; this resulted in a large demand for casual labour at picking time and busloads of pickers (mainly women), were brought in from Corby, Bedford and St Neots. Gypsies were also employed and they negotiated their rate of pay every morning before beginning work.

However, by the late 1980s, most of the vegetable crops had been phased out and the labour requirement, both regular and casual, had dwindled with the switch to cereals and combinable break crops.

In the early 1990s, Tommy Saul retired and the farms in Bedfordshire were sold. The Grange farmhouse is now privately owned and the buildings are used commercially. The land on the Riseley side is farmed by Paul Forster from Bletsoe, while Michael Whitlock from Swineshead farms the remaining ground.

*Pea viner at Grange Farm*

**Red House Farm** is to the south of Riseley on the edge of the parish, next to the Bletsoe road. The farmstead is not typical of other farms with the old buildings being mainly timber-framed and brick-infilled with pantiled roofs. The farmhouse is two storeys high, but only one brick thick; it is draughty and cold in winter according to past and present occupants, though the upper storeys have been wood-clad in recent years.

The location of the house and buildings is not covered on the Enclosure map, but the land towards Riseley was owned by Lord St John and it remained a part of this estate until relatively recently.

Fred Felce farmed at Red House in the early 1900s and his son Horace remembers, as a young schoolboy, leading horses with carts at harvest to collect loads of sheaves and looking after sheep on the harvested stubbles with his sister.

After Fred and his family moved to Riseley Lodge Farm in 1929, Red House was taken on for a time by Mr Day and his son-in-law, Ted Woodward. However, this was during the agricultural depression of the 1930s, when grain and stock did not sell well and there was no demand for the land; by the late 1930s the farm was neglected and in a poor state.

Frank Felce, Fred's brother, moved to Red House in 1939 with his sons Jack, Alf and Reg. They had come from the smallholding they farmed at 109 High Street, Riseley, and Lord St John let them have the farm rent-free for a year to try and bring it back into production.

The Felces had provided a milk round in Riseley from their smallholding and this was carried on at Red House, with Jack taking the milk round on his bicycle. The cows were mainly Shorthorn with some Friesians and were milked by hand twice a day. The farmers who supplied milk to the villagers had to stop these sales when pasteurisation was introduced, as they would have had to install a pasteurisation unit at their dairies. Pigs were also kept, with one being salted or smoked for the house and the remainder sold to dealers. In later years, sheep were kept. Work horses were bred and broken in, to use with carts and other drawn implements. On one occasion, an unbroken mare became so nervous after being harnessed into a cart for the first time, that she reared up, knocked herself out on the barn roof and broke the cart shaft!

The stock was housed during the winter months in three yards. This produced a lot of manure which had to be cleared into a heap in the yards; from here it was loaded on to carts, moved to the fields and left in small heaps about six yards apart, which then had to be spread – all by hand.

Much of the cropping was to provide animal feed, such as turnips and mangolds (wurzels), clover and sainfoin for hay and wheat, barley and oats. Straw from the cereals could be chopped through a chaff cutter for feed. This was a handworked machine, but Alf rigged up his Triumph motorbike to drive the cutter.

*Muck heaps waiting to be spread*

Savages were used with their steam engines for threshing and for cultivating. Northerns and their crawlers were contracted for ploughing and subsoiling. Italian POWs, Land Army girls and Polish refugees provided additional labour at busy times.

The farm had its first tractor during the Second World War, a standard Fordson on metal wheels. Jack remembers ploughing in the field they farmed on the Dean turn corner, north of Riseley, when, as mentioned in "In Times of War", an American B-17 bomber flew low over the tractor and crash landed in the garden of 170 High Street, ending up in the old brickyard. The plane was found to be unmanned, the crew having baled out miles before, because it was so badly damaged.

The farm had a lucky escape later in the War, when a German bomber searching for the nearby Thurleigh airfield at night dropped its bombs in Galsey Wood after seeing a light at neighbouring Bletsoe Park Farm – fortunately none of the bombs exploded!

In the early 1950s however, Red House was not so lucky when a case of foot and mouth disease was confirmed at the farm. This extremely contagious disease, which affects all cloven-hooved animals such as cattle, pigs and sheep, had first been found at Bletsoe Park Farm. All of the local farms were quarantined and the susceptible stock at any farm where the disease appeared, were slaughtered and the carcasses destroyed. Jack still remembers the terrible scenes at Red House as the animals were killed and then burned or buried.

It was during this outbreak that the farm was sold by the St John estate. Sadly, none of the Felces were able to attend the sale in order to bid to buy the farm, because of the quarantine restrictions. The farm was purchased by a Mr Robinson. Ironically, the Ministry officials overseeing the quarantine were seen at the sale!

Frank died soon after and, with no security of tenure, his sons had to leave Red House in 1954. Alf and Reg bought the farm near St Neots which Fred Clifton had just left when he moved to Harings and it is still farmed by the family. Jack and his wife stayed in Riseley and he went to work at Park Farm, Bletsoe, where he joined George Smith, who was already employed by Mr Ingle.

Mr Robinson subsequently sold Red House (now with vacant possession) to the Eastwood family who farmed Town Farm in Riseley and the two were run together. Both farms were later sold to the Joyce family, who still farm them today.

The house and buildings at Red House were sold separately from the land and are occupied by the Matthews family. Their middle son, Cris, breeds and trains polo ponies there.

**Riseley Lodge Farm** is situated towards the northern end of the village, at the end of Bowers Lane, which joins the High Street. The farmhouse dates from the 1600s and there is a range of later brick buildings behind forming stock yards. These include an 18th century timber-framed granary. Modern farm buildings have been erected behind.

The Enclosure map of 1793 shows the farm in the possession of the Duke of Bedford. However, by 1862 it was part of the St John estate, farmed by Samuel Whitehead who was also tenanting Coldham Lodge. He was succeeded by his son-in-law, Duncan Bower, after whom *'Bowers Lane'* was named.

It was during his tenancy, towards the end of the First World War, that an order was served to plough up grassland. This was objected to, but had to be carried out and there followed a compensation claim for the loss of grassland in 1919. When Duncan Bower retired, Fred Felce (who was farming at Red House at the time) was offered the tenancy of Riseley Lodge by Lord St John and he and his family moved to the farm in 1929. His son Horace is still there, along with his son Ronald and grandson Connor – a rare situation of three generations of one family actively involved in farming.

*Riseley Lodge Farm*

When Fred moved from Red House the stock was driven on foot to Riseley Lodge, this being the only way to move animals as there were no livestock lorries in those days. In later years, Len Wildman ran livestock lorries from his yard in Rotten Row until he retired and the business was taken on by Brian Tompkins (one of Arthur's sons at Town Farm) from premises near Gold Street bridge.

Despite the wartime pressure to plough out grassland, Riseley Lodge remained a mixed farm with some grass being retained today. Cattle were kept until the mid-1980s, with over 100 head at one time, and were sold through Bedford and St Neots markets. Livestock farming was not without its risks however, and tragically, Fred was killed by a bull in 1950. Grassland was rented either to graze or for making into hay. Before the Second World War, the grass at Melchbourne Park was rented and it was from here that a piece of mistletoe was brought back to Riseley Lodge, where it survives to this day.

Haymaking has always been weather dependent but in the days before *'big bales'*, mechanical handlers or even balers, it was very hard work. The earliest mowers were ground-wheel driven and pulled by a couple of horses or tractors as they became available. Once mown, the grass had to dry in the sun to make hay. It was turned with a hay rake until dry. It was then pitched in bundles by hand on to a cart, unloaded and made into a hayrick at the farm, again by hand.

*Turning hay by hand in the field that is now Riseley Playing Field*

Fred had used his first tractor, a Titan, at Red House to drive the threshing drum. When he moved to Riseley Lodge he bought a portable steam engine from Eustace Savage and this was used instead. Horace remembers being sent to the village to recruit some of the older men to come and help – Clary and Tudor Bateman, Johnny King and Jonathon Dickens. The pay was 5 shillings (25p) per day, though other casual workers would come to work at harvest for free, provided they had a drink of beer afterwards; this was brewed in the farmhouse cellar. During the War, Italian and German prisoners of war were also used. This annual event died when combine harvesters appeared and Horace bought his first one in 1951: a petrol-engined Massey Harris, which was a self-propelled bagger.

There were also several regular men who worked at Riseley Lodge: Jim Felce (Fred's nephew), Harry Barker (horse-keeper), Tommy Hales, Ted Walker and George Rootham who had injured his arm in a fall from a horse and worked part-time while also caretaking at the school. He had started on the farm as a schoolboy and worked there all his life.

*Carting hay*

Savages were used in the beginning for steam ploughing and also for cultivating the summer fallows, as a means of killing weeds in the dry summer months. A John Deere tractor was acquired during the War. While working on this one day, Horace was reminded that living near to the airfield was risky. He found himself confronted by a 100lb bomb sticking out of the field he was cultivating. It was one of several dropped from too low an altitude, preventing their fuses from detonating. Horace went to the Observer Corps post, of which he was a member, and alerted the bomb disposal squad. Bombs and live ammunition continued to be a danger long after the War finished on local farmland.

The cropping has changed over the years, in common with many farms. Wheat and barley have always been grown and in the past oats as well, with beans, clover and sugar beet. Nowadays both Riseley Lodge and Coldham Lodge, which was acquired in the 1980s, are continuous cereals.

Farming in Riseley

**Coldham Lodge Farm**, to the north-east of Riseley, is reached by a farm track running off the Swineshead road. Its name was taken from *'Coldham Close'*, an area of land mentioned in the Domesday Book.

*Coldham Lodge Farm*

This same land was acquired by the St John family in the reign of Henry VIII at the time of the Reformation and was described as *'a close pasture in Riseley called Coldham, parcel of Chicksands Priory, lately dissolved'*.

When the Enclosure survey was completed in 1793 Coldham was still in the St John name, with no house or buildings shown. However, by 1862, the brick-built farmhouse and outbuildings, still present today, are recorded and the tenant was Samuel Whitehead, who also farmed at neighbouring Riseley Lodge Farm; he was succeeded by his son-in-law, Duncan Bower. On his retirement, Fred Felce farmed it for several years after he came to Riseley Lodge.

Mr Hearn took over from the Felces and ran dairy cows in the 1930s supplying milk to the village. One of his employees was George Smith, who had also worked at Riseley Lodge and he remained until Mr Hearn's death, when the farm was sold to Mr North.

T A Saul bought the farm in the 1950s and ran it alongside his other newly acquired farms at Riseley Grange, Eastfields and Melchbourne Grange, under the management of John Merriken and later Jim Turnbull. When T A Saul sold his farms in the 1980s, Coldham was again taken on by the Felce family at Riseley Lodge Farm and is still farmed by them today.

**Town Farm** is found at the southern end of Riseley High Street. The brick-built farmhouse is now privately owned and in the process of being renovated. It dates back to the late 1700s with two storeys and an old tile roof, being an example of a more prosperous farm of the time which started as a small house and was then extended. The range of old farm buildings has also been sold and converted into private houses. The old barn on the corner of Lowsdon Lane is the most noteworthy, with a timber frame and brick in-filling dating back to the 1700s.

The modern farm buildings are situated behind the old farmyard and are reached from Lowsdon Lane.

*Town Farm House*

On the Enclosure survey, the farm is in the name of Peter Creale and as it is not shown in the St John estate records of 1862, it would appear that the farm was freehold. In the late 1800s it was farmed by Mr Harris, whose wife, Anne, was the daughter of Jonathon Blott from Daintry Farm in the village. It was sold to David Waldock in the 1880s who also bought Lowsdown and Tidbury Farms and ran the three holdings together. He married the daughter of the Smiths from High Barn House and their daughter Margaret Waldock now 93, was teacher at the village school for many years.

David Waldock ran a mixed farm with cereals and root crops alongside the grass on which he ran cattle and sheep. The cows were milked and Town Farm was one of several farms supplying milk and butter to the village. Milking in those days was done by hand into buckets and there was no treatment apart from straining before storing in churns. If butter was needed, the milk was poured into large pans where it remained until the cream had risen. Once set, it was skimmed off and stored in earthenware crocks in the cooler house dairy before having salt added, being hand churned and patted into butter. The remaining milk was sold as 'skimmed' milk, normal milk was full cream, of course.

Horses were used for the majority of jobs around the farm and there was a man employed as horse keeper who arrived for work at 6.00 am, in order to feed, water and groom the horses ready for the rest of the men at 7.00 am.

The crops grown included many for animal feed, such as oats, barley, potatoes and mangolds as well as forage crops such as clover which was cut and stored in stacks – the clover stack one year was enormous, and is still talked about.

Machinery was increasingly being used, with steam engine contractors being employed to plough and cultivate the ground and to thresh the corn. David Waldock used a contractor called Mr Hooker from Milton Ernest, who used to come to the farm to buy butter.

David died in 1933 from influenza and his son Henry sold the farm to the Eastwood family, but stayed on as manager. He married Winifred Howard from Daintry Farm, sister to Jack and Wally and granddaughter of Jonathon Blott.

The Eastwoods were in the meat trade, importing cattle from Ireland and Canada and bringing them to Town Farm for quarantine via Bedford and Sharnbrook Stations. They also kept pigs in the farm buildings, as well as maintaining the sheep flock.

Riseley – Our Village

*The clover stack - Town Farm*
*Top to bottom (left to right): Henry Millard (on leave from the Canadian Army), Harry Smith, Isobel Collins, Sam Wildman, Sophie Ball, Tom Clayton, Rhodda Sharman, Ernest Ball, Henry Waldock, Margaret Waldock, Mabel Ball, Sylvia Williamson*

Tractors were beginning to appear, though steam tackle was still being used.  The farm still had work for five or six men because of the large numbers of stock.  Ken Rootham was pigman, Jim Hancock was still looking after the remaining horses, George Smith, Ken Spavins, Eric Ellis and Tony Cerasale were also employed.  Tony had started work on the farm *'officially'* in 1947 when he left school and still works there today, having collected 40 and 50 year long-service medals from the Royal Agricultural Society.  He remembers very clearly the War years, when the Americans were based at the new airfield at Thurleigh which the farm bordered (it had lost a lot of land when the airfield was built).  There was no perimeter fence then and the farm ran right up to the dispersal points and the firing ranges.  Test firing was normally ignored but on one occasion, as mentioned in "In Times of War" Tony was harrowing near to the planes when someone fired right over the top of his head from one of the aeroplane gun turrets - he packed up and went home!

It was also common at harvest time to find burnt circles in the crops, where enemy planes had dropped incendiary bombs – intended for the airfield – which had gone off and burnt a small area of the damp corn during the night.

After the War, Eastwoods bought the land of neighbouring College Farm from Albert Sharman. In 1953, with the retirement of Henry Waldock, Arthur Tompkins was appointed manager and brought his family to Town Farm.  The Eastwoods subsequently sold the farm in 1973 to the Joyce family who farmed at Renhold.

The arrival of Arthur Tompkins and the Joyce family resulted in some sweeping changes.  The stock was cut right back, apart from some sheep which were kept until quite recently, and the fields became predominantly arable.  More cereals were grown with most of the straw being burnt as there was less demand from animals.

Mechanisation improved with better diesel tractors being used.  Initially, contractors such as Northerns from Harrold were employed with crawlers, but later the farm carried out all its own cultivations.  Combines were becoming more common and a tractor-towed bagger was hired to begin with, before a more modern combine with a bulk tank was bought.

The farm buildings were modernised with storage sheds and a bulk grain handling plant with silos and a drier being added.

The 1970s brought the introduction of a new break crop for the rotation: oilseed rape. This soon became a common sight with its bright yellow fields at flowering time. Potatoes were no longer grown and barley was replaced with more wheat. Cultivations changed from the plough to a minimal approach, where the soil was lightly worked after the straw was burnt, then the seed drilled. The emphasis had swung away from the traditional mix of crops with autumn and spring sowings to autumn sown wheat and oilseed rape, typical of most of the local farms at this time. However, with the ban on straw burning in 1993 and the resulting problems with weed control, the plough has returned to many farms.

*Stubble burning – Martin Harris at Grange Farm*

With the retirement of Arthur Tompkins in 1989, the Joyce's youngest nephew Jeremy Markham took over the management at Town Farm and has steered it into the 21st century with the help of Tony and one other full-time employee.

**Tidbury and Lowsdown Farms** were both to the far south-east of Riseley on the boundary of the parish with Bletsoe and Thurleigh.

Lowsdown Farm was almost a mile away from the village and could be reached by a cart track extending from what is now Lowsdon Lane.

On the Enclosure map of 1793 it is recorded to an Isaac Field, but is not referred to on the 1862 St John estate map. The last tenants in the 19th century were Mr Belton followed by Mr Carrington and then Charles Felce, who also owned the smallholding at 109 High Street and moved to Radwell when the farm was sold to David Waldock in 1898.

The yard and house at Lowsdown were always derelict within living memory, although the farmhouse would have been impressive in its day, being a large two-storey timber-framed H-plan dwelling (similar to The Fox and Hounds public house). Built in the late 1600s, it had integral fireplaces with brick chimney stacks and may well have been brick in-filled from the beginning. There was an orchard at the farm and two very deep ponds – one for animals and the other fenced off for the house.

Tidbury Farm was over a mile away as the crow flies, and was probably reached by another cart track extending from Galsey Lane, which ran along the northern edge of Galsey Wood. The buildings and house were used at Tidbury in the late 1800s with chickens and hens being kept and a farmworker by the name of Alderman Franklin living in the old farmhouse. In the summer, *'Tidbury Feast'* was the time when the shearing gang from Town Farm penned sheep in the yard and clipped their fleeces. People remember an old lady, known as *'Tidbury Liz'*, living at the farm and walking down to the village, but no-one knows how she came to be there.

The farm was owned by a Cambridge college from whom it was let to David Waldock. On the Enclosure map it is referred to as *'College Farm*

*Tedbury'*. Like Lowsdown, it seems that it never belonged to the St John estate. It was bought, along with Lowsdown Farm, by David Waldock in the late 1800s. He had bought Town Farm earlier and now ran the three farms together.

*Hand shearing with stack behind – Joe Smith ('Fuge') and Aubrey Savage*

With the outbreak of the Second World War, Thurleigh airfield was built. This resulted in Tidbury farmstead being demolished as it was in the middle of the new airfield and much of the land from Tidbury and Lowsdown was lost. The remains of the orchard can still be seen at the old Lowsdown Farm, but the buildings and ponds were removed long ago.

**Lord's Farm** is no longer in existence, but reference has been found in old records to indicate that its most likely location was to the north of Rotten Row. The farmhouse was the large white dwelling which used to be 12, 14 and 16 Rotten Row. This house dates from the 17th century and is one of the large T-plan timber-framed farmhouses of that period, notable for their integral fireplaces.

In 1793, the house and 130 acres of land were sold by Elizabeth Bletsoe to Thomas Gell and his brother Richard. Thomas was a yeoman, who owned or rented various properties and pieces of land in Riseley. Richard was an innkeeper. Their descendants still live in the village. The Enclosure map of the same year shows the house and the land behind it in Thomas Gell's name.

In 1802 it was leased to the churchwardens and overseers of the parish as a workhouse; this further strengthens the case for its location in Rotten Row, because this property was always known as the site of the old workhouse, though no-one remembers its existence.

Thomas Gell subsequently sold Lord's Farm to the Duke of Bedford. It later came into the St John estate and the land was amalgamated with neighbouring Lodge Farm. The farmhouse was converted into three cottages and was sold with the break-up of the estate in 1951, being purchased by the Wallis family. Part of the house is now privately owned.

**Parkers Farm** is similar to Lord's Farm in several ways: it is no longer in existence as a farm and records show that it was once owned by Thomas Gell. In 1793 he and his brother Richard bought *'Parkers farmhouse, other dwellings and twenty acres of common fields'*.

The farmhouse was probably the same building as The Fox and Hounds public house which is known to be a good example of a large, H-plan farmhouse built in the early 1600s. This is further confirmed by the Enclosure map of 1793 which shows the house and the land behind it in Thomas Gell's name.

The farm was later sold by the Gells to the Duke of Bedford. Nowadays, it is owned by the Charles Wells brewery and has the added interest of once being the home of the Taylor family, who were famous bell founders.

**Daintry Farm** was one of the larger smallholdings in the village. It was situated halfway along the High Street on the north-west side, just past the modern day shop and Post Office. The farmhouse (number 95) was built in the 18th century and is now privately owned. The remains of the old farmyard can still be seen behind the house with the entrance directly off the High Street.

In 1793 it was farmed by William Bonfield. By 1862 it was part of the St John estate and the tenant was Thomas Gell. However, the land was sold and Jonathon Blott came to live at the farm from Raunds. It was mostly down to grass at this time and he milked cows and sold milk to the village. He also kept pigs and work horses for the arable land he rented on Mill Hill - now Keysoe Road. The fields behind the farm ran either side of the brook and up to the church. Jonathon did not farm the glebe (church) fields but he did give some ground to extend the churchyard.

On Jonathon's death his daughter Priscilla persuaded her brother to let her have the farm. She married Walter Howard and they remained in Riseley. Priscilla's sister Anne was also involved with farming in the village after marrying Mr Harris at Town Farm.

Walter and Priscilla's son Arthur John (Jack) (who had quite a reputation with his shotgun!) carried on with the farm in Riseley. His brother Walter Blott (Wally) Howard, a noted athlete, went to Brook Farm, Ravensden and their sister Winifred (Cissie) married Henry Waldock at Town Farm, Riseley.

Jack Howard married Peggie, daughter of a dairy farmer in Buckinghamshire, and they farmed Daintry. Peggie remembers the farm name being given to them during the Second World War because all farms had to be identified. They were still milking cows, Friesians by now as opposed to the more common Shorthorn breed, selling the milk in the village and because of this were allowed to keep the grass. They also ran sheep and kept pigs which were sold at Bedford market. Jack kept working horses and used them for ploughing and other jobs, but he contracted Savages engines and drum to thresh his corn. When Jack retired in the late 1970s the farm was rented to their neighbour, Cyril Clayton.

**Hillview Farm**
Cyril came to Riseley in the 1950s when he bought Dorville House on the corner of Keysoe Road and the land behind it. His family had originally farmed at Thurleigh, but the farm had lost some ground when the airfield was built in 1940 and then the remaining land plus the

farmhouse were taken when the runway was extended in 1952.

Initially, he kept free-range hens, pigs, a few cattle and grew mainly brussels and potatoes with runner beans and cereals to be fed to the stock; an animal mix was sown, known as dredge corn, comprising of oats, wheat, barley, peas and beans.

The vegetable crops had a high labour requirement and two regular men were employed for brussels while casual local labour (mainly women) was used for potatoes. Falling returns from these crops led to a reduction in the numbers employed. The farm now relies predominantly on family labour from Cyril's son Graham and grandson Sam, with Cyril taking more of a back seat. Here, again, are three generations involved in farming.

The cropping now centres more on cereals and oilseed rape, but some vegetables are still grown and sold from the farm shop off the Keysoe Road.

The church ground around the churchyard was taken on in the 1980s and this is run alongside Jack Howard's land.

In recent years, Dorville House was sold and the new farmstead at Hillview was built behind.

**High Barn House** is to be found on the north side of the High Street, near to Gold Street bridge and opposite The Five Bells public house, reached by a private bridge over the brook. It is an example of a 17th century T-plan timber-framed farmhouse, with various extensions added in the 18th and 19th centuries.

The house was originally the farmhouse to High Barn Farm, which is on the Sharnbrook road nearly half a mile to the south-west of Riseley. Why the holding and house were so far apart is a mystery, although High Barn House did have its own range of brick and timber-framed buildings surrounding a stockyard. They both belonged to the St John estate and the tenant, William Whitehead, is named in both of them in 1862.

Riseley – Our Village

*High Barn House*

There were a couple of small fields that belonged to High Barn House and by the time the Smith family (whose daughter married David Waldock at Town Farm) lived there in the late 1800s, it was run as a smallholding separate from the farm at High Barn.

Fred King followed the Smiths in 1911, initially as tenant, but eventually as owner. He and his family kept pigs and dairy cows, delivering milk to Sharnbrook village and selling to local people at the farm door, as well as running the Post Office. Fred employed several local men including George Smith, Tom Farrar and Albert Sharman. George Smith worked at the smallholding from leaving school at 14 until he was 16 years old, when Fred King let him go because he did not want to pay his National Insurance Stamp – a common practice among local farmers.

Albert Sharman started work for Fred at 13 years of age. Now 91, he remembers fetching the cows from Cuckoo Fields at the end of Dag Lane for milking at High Barn House – a job he did, by hand, before school. He also remembers receiving a beating from Mr Hewitt the headmaster for being late, despite explaining that he had been helping to calve a cow. When Fred King heard about this he *'had a word'* with the headmaster, who never dared to punish Albert again – even though he was late on many occasions!

Most of the work was still carried out by hand. The corn at harvest was cut with a sickle or scythe, tied into a sheaf with a straw band and stacked in groups of eight to ten sheaves called shocks. These were left to dry in the field before being collected by horse and cart and taken to the farm rickyard and stacked to await threshing. In a full day a mowing gang could cut, tie and stack about an acre per man (which is the size of a football pitch) with the various jobs being swapped around to give breaks.

*Mowing gang, circa 1900*

The arrival of the reaper, which cut the corn mechanically and left it in untied bundles, and then later the binder, which tied the cut corn into sheaves, were greeted with much enthusiasm. However, Albert and nearly all the older farmers remember the introduction of the combine harvester as the most significant agricultural advance in their lifetime. With one machine, the corn could be cut, threshed and stored (initially in bags and later in bulk), drastically reducing the number of men and hours of work needed to do the same jobs. Today, one man on an average combine with another carting the grain can harvest 2-3 acres an hour, with larger capacity machines doing much more.

*Horse drawn binder*

Horses were employed extensively and Albert remembers ploughing about an acre a day with three horses pulling one furrow and later four or five pulling two furrows. They were also used to pull harrows after the plough, as well as the seed drill, to pull the reaper or binder and any carting jobs with hay, corn sheaves, or muck.

The introduction of tractors was a gradual process, with many farmers unable to afford them and others working them alongside horses and steam engines. The first tractors were quite crude affairs, running on petrol (to start them) and paraffin (TVO - tractor vaporising oil). They were started with a crank handle, had no batteries and therefore no lights. Landwork stopped at dark or carried on by moonlight.

Albert's first tractor, a Fordson with iron wheels, needed covers over the grips or *'spuds'* to enable it to run on the road.

Albert married Fred King's daughter Kate and they ran High Barn House along with College Farm, which Albert had purchased from his neighbour Clary Bateman. Kate and her sister Francis King subsequently sold the farm, and the house is now privately owned. The land was built on and is now *'The Orchard'*. They also sold some outlying land along Church Lane where the council houses, flats and garages were built in *'King's Close'*.

*Combine harvesters at Grange Farm*

**College Farm** is no longer in existence, but used to be on the north-west side of the High Street near to where the police station is now. Unusually for Riseley, the farmhouse was stone built. The farm buildings were behind the house and were comprised of brick and timber buildings, forming two stockyards (one for cattle and horses, the other for pigs). There was some land around the farmyard, with the remainder alongside the Bedford road to the south-east of Riseley.

Early records show the farm belonging to Corpus Christi College in Oxford, who rented it out on lease agreements. At the time of the Enclosures in 1793 the leasehold was in the name of William Burbridge. By 1846 it was held by the Todd family, left in the will of Francis Todd to his nephew Richard *'a farmhouse, cottage barn and outbuildings with about 76 acres leased from Chrispus College at Oxford'*. William Rootham farmed after the Todd family and in living memory, Alfred Linford was at College Farm at the turn of the 19th century, followed by Mr Green who managed the farm for a Mr Pitts. Many people remember Clary Bateman, the next tenant. He kept a lot of chickens, many of them in home-made roosts of straw and wood along the Bedford road, which were regularly raided by foxes. This was not a major disaster as any losses to foxes (that could be accounted for), were paid by the local hunt.

Clary bought College Farm from Corpus Christi College and subsequently sold it to Albert Sharman who ran it with High Barn House and his other pieces of ground around the village and along the Sharnbrook road. After the Second World War, the land along the Bedford road was sold to the Eastwoods at neighbouring Town Farm. The house, farmstead and surrounding fields were later sold for building, resulting in the estates of College Drive, Wells and Brooklands Roads. Sadly, College Farmhouse was demolished in January 1965, but a photograph survives.

*College Farm House from the High Street with High Barn House in the background*

**109 High Street** is found between what was The Royal Oak public house and the Chapel Gallery. The plot of land behind runs down to the brook.

It is now a private house, but at the turn of the 19th century was owned by Charles Felce who lived at Radwell. He had previously rented Lowsdown Farm before moving and rented 109 to his brother, Frank; Fred, another brother, farmed at Red House Farm and later at Riseley Lodge Farm.

Frank's son Jack remembers keeping pigs, cattle and working horses at the smallholding, in the old sheds behind the house. Grass and arable fields were farmed at various locations around the village: Mill Hill, Dean turn and the glebe land around the church was rented.

The cows were handmilked and a recognised milk round was operated around Riseley. Butter was made and kept in a cold cellar at Fred Wise's house, the other side of The Royal Oak. A sweet shop was also run from the house.

In 1939, Frank and his family moved to Red House to take on the tenancy and Charles sold 109 to Mr Dewsbery. He kept Shorthorn cattle in the fields on Mill Hill (Keysoe Road) and milked them by machine in the cowshed at 109; there was a cooler installed in the milk line and he sold the milk to the dairy in churns. Hens were also kept in battery cages and the eggs sold.

In 1972, Mr Dewsbery sold the house, land and Keysoe Road fields to David Chapman. He kept beef cattle at Keysoe Road and pigs at 109, where he replaced the milking parlour with farrowing crates. The progeny were fattened on site and later sold, along with home-produced beef and lamb, from the butchers and farm shop David opened at 109.

In 1988, David sold 109 High Street and built a new house and pig unit on the Keysoe Road, named *'Mill Pond'*. Here he runs sows outside and fattens their progeny, producing pigs to a very high standard. It is one of the few pig units still operating locally following one of the longest periods of depression in the pig industry.

**71 High Street** was built and lived in by Ralph Savage when he married and was named *'Invicta House'* after one of the makes of his steam engines. He oversaw the running of the family's steam contracting business by two of his sons – Eustace and Roland – and paid the men every Saturday evening from his office at 71.

His other son, Aubrey, farmed at High Barn but lost the tenancy on Ralph's death. He and his family moved into 71 in the 1950s and Aubrey ran a smallholding there until his death in the 1980s.

He kept sows and fattened pigs in the old farm buildings next to the house, with hens and geese running free range in the two fields, one on either side of the Brook: fat pigs, eggs and honey were sold.

When Aubrey died, 71 was sold and is now privately owned. The old buildings were demolished and new houses built to create *'The Barns'*.

**15 Gold Street** is the northern end of the two semi-detached houses on the south side of Gold Street. It is now privately owned, but was once part of the St John estate along with the grass field behind, which extended up to Rotten Row.

Bani Rootham kept milking cows at the smallholding and is remembered by older residents.

Miss Waldock was tenant after Bani and lived in the house while teaching at the village school; Len Williams kept pigs in the yard behind at the same time, and also rented three arable fields at the end of Dag Lane from Lord St John.

The house, land behind and the arable fields were all sold by the St John estate in the 1950s. The Dag Lane fields were bought by Peter Wilkinson at Sackville Lodge Farm, while Miss Waldock and Len remained at Gold Street. Part of the grass field behind 15 Gold Street, with road frontage, was subsequently sold to Walt Walker, who built a small area of glasshouses and a bungalow next to Rotten Row. He ran a nursery until he sold up to a developer who demolished the nursery and bungalow and eventually built three new houses on Rotten Row and one in the middle of the grass field behind.

**Shackles Field** is the last remaining smallholding in Riseley on Rotten Row. It is kept by Aubrey Felce who still has some poultry and runs a vegetable stall, noted for its strawberries in the summer.

Shackles Field and the adjacent Soot Pyckle, were farmed by Jim Felce (Aubrey's father), who also rented the glebe land and a grass field at the end of Gold Street and Dag Lane, since built on. He also tenanted and then bought from Lord St John the site of the redundant allotments, known as Clay Mount on the Bedford road. This was one of several

Farming in Riseley

*Threshing straw for the thatch at High Barn House, 1971. Ted Pentlow (far left) and Bob Pentlow (far right)*

fields around the village where people could rent an allotment to grow food for themselves or to sell. Some allotments were larger and were used to grow cereals. The harvested sheaves were then stacked in a communal rick, before everyone gathered for the threshing with drum and steam engine. Many of these allotments were derelict in the 1930s, until the War brought them back into production.

Jim Felce worked for his uncle (Fred Felce) at Red House and Riseley Lodge Farms and ran the other land as a smallholding with dairy cows, pigs, arable crops (for feed and bedding straw) and vegetables. Jim and his family had lived in a cottage with a yard and outbuildings towards the Gold Street end of Rotten Row, where a bungalow now stands. They subsequently moved to The White Horse, where his wife May managed the pub. They had taken over when Mrs Beeby, the previous landlady, had left.

Jim's son Aubrey carried on with pigs on Rotten Row until quite recently and still keeps his vegetable stall stocked, although he and his wife Phyllis are now retired. The glebe land was given up in the 1980s, Clay Mount was sold and is now used for horse paddocks and Shackles Field has recently been built on.

---

*Did you know that . . .*

*A couple of villagers have found the remains of what are believed to be Roman kilns in their back gardens.*

# Earning a Living
Andrew Gell

## The Windmills

Although Riseley is recorded as having two windmills in the parish, the only one still working as a mill into the 1900s was the four bladed post mill situated at the top of the hill on the Keysoe Road, known to older villagers as Mill Lane or Mill Hill. Two of the sails were covered with canvas and two were single row wooden shutters. The sails were 55 feet long from tip to tip. Having two sets of sails fitted with wooden shutters (similar in function to venetian blinds) reduced the power the mill would have produced if both sets of sails were covered in canvas. The advantage was that if there were any sudden changes in the speed of the wind, it would force the wooden shutters partly open thereby spilling part of the wind and keeping the mill running at a steady speed. A sudden increase in the wind with just canvas-sheeted sails would have meant stopping the mill and reefing in the canvas. With the changes in British weather and the deliberate siting of the windmills in exposed locations, the Riseley design was a very labour saving device.

*The Keysoe Road windmill*

Some of the millers recorded were Robert Rootham in 1848, Richard Simpson in 1869 and in the year leading up to its closure in 1916, Charles Woodward, Benjamin Rootham and Daniel Rootham. Daniel was the last recorded miller. The miller lived in 82 High Street, which is today called Old Mill Cottage.

Following its closure in 1916 the mill fell into general disrepair and in 1938 was just a shell with the canvas-covered sails left in place. It was struck by lightning in 1947 and caught fire. It was pulled down, as it was so unsafe. Some of the remaining woodwork was used to make a bonfire at the top of the hill for the Coronation in 1953.

There is an amusing story relating to the mill, which is about a sack of corn falling off a cart at the bottom of Mill Hill. Three locals bet another man 2d (approximately 1p) each that he could not carry the sack of corn to the top of Mill Hill. The sacks were large in those days and weighed 18 stone. Joe Smith accepted the bet and carried the sack on his shoulders up the hill and to the mill. Getting there, he shouted up to the miller to ask where the bag was required. For devilment, the miller asked for it to be brought to the top of the mill. Without pausing, Joe climbed the steps right to the top, setting the sack down with such a jolt that it shook the mill. The three paid their 2d to Joe and they all made their way to The Royal Oak, to have a drink on the strength of Joe's achievement.

Riseley's second windmill was on the site of the glasshouses owned by the Vincent family on the Swineshead road. As mentioned in "Farming in Riseley", it is known as Mill Farm Nursery, the cottage adjacent being Mill Cottage. The brick foundations are still there, but although there is no record of when it actually closed, it was certainly before the end of the 19th century. None of the names of the millers are documented, but the last was believed to be Joshua Hunt.

In addition to the two windmills, the village had a wholesale flour merchant whose premises were at Hall Farm, 133 High Street. He was Mr Harris and his business closed sometime in the late 1920s.

## Building Trades

Unlike today, Riseley was virtually self-sufficient in the building trades – even down to the provision of the basic building materials. The village had its own brickyard, which operated from 1558 to its closure in 1874. Adjacent to the brickyard was a tile yard where roof tiles were made. These two industries occupied the land from Bowers Lane, starting behind the cottages in Waldocks Close, to 170 High Street. The clay excavation workings are still clearly to be seen, although all the buildings are gone.

The owner of the brick and tile yards was Lord St John of Bletsoe, from Melchbourne House, until they were sold to the Paine family in 1848. James Paine came from the St Neots brewing family who owned The George and Dragon public house where Waldocks Close is now. They remained with the Paine family until their closure, through James' son William who bought the yard for £170 in 1856-57.

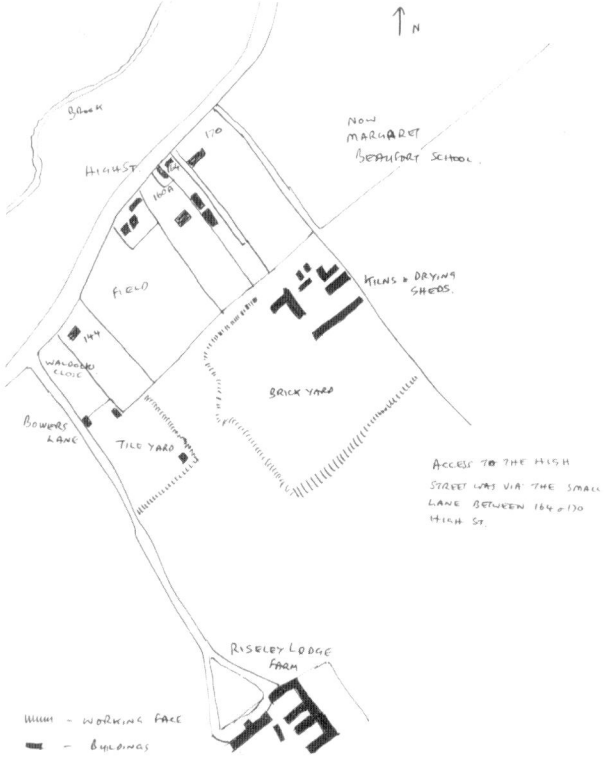

*Diagram of the layout of the brickyard and tile yard*

The locally made Riseley brick is very distinctive and its heyday was the mid-1800s when most of the local farmhouses were built. The bricks are easily identified by the orange and yellow chequerboard effect when the bricks are laid. The different colours were not due to any difference in the clay, but to the positioning of the bricks in the kilns. The different temperatures caused the difference in colour.

The traditional name for a Riseley brick is a Riseley Black Heart. Anyone who has tried to break one in half, or tried to drill into it, will testify as to the hardness of the black centre.

*109 High Street in typical Riseley brick. At the time of this photograph it was a shop run by Martha Felce*

At the top end of the village where Cedarbrook stands and along Lowsdon Lane were the two village sand-pits. Both were owned by Lord St John before being sold to private individuals. Sand was excavated behind Cedarbrook as late as the late 1950s. Sam Williamson, the local builder and bricklayer who lived at 4 High Street, owned the sand-pit up Lowsdon Lane.

There is a record in the Parish Council minutes of 1900 of lime pits in the field where College Drive is now. The lime was essential for building. Unfortunately, no records have yet been found to confirm when the lime pits were in operation. Older residents can remember the fenced pits, but not lime being dug. Alfred Linford farmed College Farm at the end of the 1800s and he may have operated the lime pits.

Unlike the villages across the A6 and into Northamptonshire, Riseley has not much construction in stone. However, in the old cottages constructed mainly of wattle and daub, there was a need for the chimney breasts to be of a fireproof material. Most of the older cottages, pre 1800, have stone built chimney breasts and some have stone in their shallow foundations. This stone was excavated from earthworks at Stone Pit Close, which is visible from the Swineshead road across the fields on the left, opposite the sewage works. It is now largely covered in trees and bushes, but is quite a deep excavation. Unfortunately, we have no specific dates as to when this was operating and when it closed down.

With this supply of basic building materials the local tradesmen could build a complete house from foundation to roof.

In 1900 some of the tradesmen operating in the village were:- **Thomas Williamson**, the local builder and bricklayer. Some of the brick buildings at Lodge Farm have TW engraved in the bricks. His son Samuel carried on after him into the 1950s. He was affectionately called Sam Wimp. **Isaac Dickens** is also recorded as a bricklayer.

**James Croot** was the plumber, painter and decorator. His son **Oscar Croot** followed on from him. He lived at 103 High Street until his death in 1963.

**William Dennis** and **William Farrar** were both carpenters. The village thatcher was **Mr Dunkley** who lived at Swan Cottage. He thatched until just after World War Two. **Roger Evans** is now the local thatcher and his skill is much in demand.

*Oscar Croot in front of Lodge Farm*

Another of the rural trades was that of **woodsman**.

*A very early photograph of woodsmen working on the St John estate*

**Tradesmen**
Riseley had shops for most goods. It was only for special items that could not be bought locally that residents made journeys to Bedford and surrounding towns.

Mrs Gell recalls that her mother, Amelia Rootham, only went to Bedford once a year to buy clothes and materials, generally from Braggins (now Beale's). There was a *'clothing club'* in the village where villagers paid weekly sums according to what they could afford. It was run by the vicar who kept all the entries recorded in cash books. Once a year, in August or September, it was paid out to the members and the ladies of the village then made their trip to Bedford to spend it.

There were also travelling shops and salesmen that called. In the 1920s a man came once a week from Bedford with a motorcycle and sidecar, selling all types of fancy cakes. Riseley was not connected to the electricity grid until just after World War Two and villagers used paraffin in oil lamps to light their houses. A man from Dean delivered paraffin.

When electricity did come, it was expensive and only the more well off had it connected. Quite a few villagers had husbands or friends who were able to do the work themselves. Mrs Di Folco recalls that her husband put the electricity in at 156 High Street, but only the lighting. She waited another three years before he wired in the electric cooker! Mrs Gell still has her invoice for wiring the complete house. It is dated 30 December 1950. The work was done by Henry Bacchus of Bedford, and the cost was £23 19s 0d (£23.95), the equivalent of about 5 weeks pay for an agricultural worker at the time.

Martins of Duke Street in Bedford came around once a fortnight selling clothes. They offered payment on easy terms and collected the instalments when they came round. Miss Barber was their long-standing representative in Riseley.

Before World War Two, the daily milk was provided by local dairy herds. Jack Howard of Daintry Farm delivered his farm milk to parts of the village, as did Jack Felce from Red House Farm. Mr Hurn of Coldham Lodge Farm also delivered. Many villagers had a cow or cows and sold their surplus milk. Mr Tarry, landlord of The Five Bells, sold milk and he had some of the first pasteurising equipment in the village. Mr Dewsbery of 109 High Street was another farmer who sold milk. His fields were up Keysoe Road and his cattle walking up and down the High Street twice a day was a regular feature of the village scene in the 1950s and 1960s. Albert Sharman was another supplier of milk from High Barn Farm House. His cattle were kept in Kings Meadow where Kings Close now stands and they were walked down Church Lane and Gold Street to be milked.

When the Co-op became established they began deliveries to the village from Rushden and the milk supply by the local village farms declined. The Co-op deliveries started sometime during World War Two.

A firm called Clarkes of Rushden came once a week to deliver newly charged accumulators and collect those that needed re-charging. The accumulator was used pre-electricity days to run the wireless and was basically a lead acid battery for heating the valves. The cost was only a few pence.

Prior to Clarkes coming round, Fred Litchfield who lived in Rotten Row used to provide the service using a mobile generator. Fred's nickname was Dofred because he used to talk to himself, saying *'Fred must do this, Fred must do that . . .'*

The village had travelling fish and chip vans twice a week; Bayes of Bedford and Wrens from Eynesbury, St Neots.

Walls ice-cream van came round in the 1950s and 1960s on a Friday and Boswells Ices came round on a Sunday morning. The sound of the chimes would attract the attention of adults and children alike.

Fresh meat was provided by Don Mole from Rushden during the Second World War, until the shop closed in the 1970s. Helletts of Kimbolton started deliveries on a Saturday from the early 1960s and still do deliver.

Fresh fish was delivered by Goodes on a Thursday for many years. Of course, the fish had to be eaten the same day as so few people had refrigerators.

In addition to these regular tradesmen there were the occasional ones who called two or three times a year selling carpets, millinery from

Luton, underwear from a man in Leicester - yes, salesmen really did travel in ladies underwear!

**Shops in Riseley**
Mrs Ginny Steers had a shop in the thatched cottage next to The Five Bells. She sold sweets, cigarettes and tobacco and non-perishable goods. When she retired in the 1960s, Mr and Mrs Middleton took it over and sold similar items as well as fancy goods and children's toys, including Matchbox toys.

Fred Litchfield (Dofred) had a shop on Gold Street bridge where Bridge House is. He sold sweets and liquorice and similar items and, again, non-perishable foods like tea, rice and flour.

Mr Ernest Valentine at Field House was a retail and wholesale trader in fruit and vegetables. He had a large barn from where he sold the produce that he bought from local farmers and markets.

Sarah Savage had her shop next to Brook House. It is apparent from the large windows, that it was a shop. She sold fancy goods and sweets. Local children were regularly seen looking at her window displays, especially when there was new stock in. During World War Two Mr and Mrs Seebon moved to the village and they then took over the shop and ran it until it closed in the late 1960s.

Granny Litchfield sold sweets and haberdashery from her front room at Brook Cottage.

Mr and Mrs Will Litchfield sold fruit and vegetables and groceries from their shop, next door to the Wesleyan Chapel in the High Street – basically just the two front rooms of the house.

The Post Office used to be run by Mrs King, High Barn House, 39 High Street. Then, in 1945 Mrs Edith Westley from Hall Cottage, 133 High Street, opened a Post Office in her back room. The entrance was via the side door and there was a hand bell to ring for attention. Our present Post Office is combined with a general store run by the Batelys. Mrs Bately took over the Post Office in June 1968. (Taken over by the Stewards in November 2000.)

Before the Batelys took over the general store, it was owned by Mr Wilf Matthews from Sharnbrook. Before him there were a succession of owners including Mr Ricketts and Mr Rousham.

*A High Street scene showing Ricketts' shop – taken about 1935*

Mrs Martha Felce had a shop in her front room at 109 High Street – now Millbrook House. There was a display window and she sold sweets and dried goods.

The Co-op opened a shop in 1938 opposite where Dodds Close is now. It was a wooden building and was very popular as the Co-op gave the '*divi*' – a dividend of 1s in the pound (5p in the pound) to be paid out once a year. The Riseley Co-op was run from the East Northants Co-op in Rushden. The Co-op closed and was dismantled in 1992.

**Shoe Trades**
Riseley was closely associated with the shoe manufacturing trades in Rushden. There were at least two small businesses making parts for shoes. The parts for the shoes would be brought out from Rushden, for people to complete. Then the finished shoes were collected. One

business was run by Joseph Gell from Cobblestones. The part of the house end on to the road was just a timber barn, which was used as the workshop. Before the First World War 17 men were employed there.

*Riseley Co-op*

Another business making up shoe components, was run on the same basis from a black shed in Keysoe Road. This had closed before World War One and the whole barn was moved to the opposite side of the road, where it became the forge and repair workshop for Savage's ploughing and threshing contracting business.

A firm at Kimbolton used the Riseley Reading Rooms, which stood at the entrance to the Barns and have now been demolished, for stitching shoe components. It operated for about three years in the 1950s before the work was transferred to a factory in Kimbolton.

Factories from Rushden continued to bring shoe components for people to complete in their own homes until the 1950s. This was the end of cottage industry in Riseley.

A Mr Portingale was a leather worker and shoe repairer working in barns in Gold Street. He then worked from the small outbuilding at

58 High Street before moving to 86 High Street, where he continued until the early 1960s.

*The Riseley Reading Rooms*

**Butchers**

There were two butchers in Riseley in 1900 and they were Mr Wyant and Son who traded from premises where 29 High Street is today and Ebeneezer Smith who had his premises at 3 Gold Street. When Ebeneezer ceased his business, Russ Warren took over. It is just still possible to make out where his painted name was on the end gable of the house. Russ Warren ceased being a butcher in the mid-1950s and Riseley lost its last butcher.

**Bakers**

There were three bakers. These not only supplied the village with bread but also for a small charge allowed villagers to use their large ovens for cooking the Sunday joints. Most village cottages just had small coal or wood fired ranges for cooking.

The bakers were Stephen Stevens who baked at The Old Swan and in the buildings that look on to the jitty next to 110/114 High Street. His son George carried on after him and also baked and sold fancy cakes from the house where Yew Trees, 56 High Street, now stands.

From the bakery next to the blacksmiths where 64 and 66 High Street stand today, Thomas Valentine worked. His house and the bakehouse were knocked down in the early 1960s and the new houses built. Tom Valentine also operated a carriers business with a horse and cart, which could be used for taking and collecting goods from the local towns and markets. It could also be hired by the day on a *'self-drive'* basis if required. Joseph Gell used to hire the cart to go to the market at Thrapston every two months. In 1879 it was recorded that Tom Valentine did a regular run to and from Bedford on Tuesday and Friday of every week. James Wadsworth, the other carrier in Riseley, went on Wednesdays and Saturdays and Samuel Wise who was a beer retailer did carrying to Bedford on Wednesdays and Saturdays also.

The third bakery was run by Alfred King and was on the site where the new houses at Litchfield stand today. Mr Ganderton took over the bakery from Mr King and ran it until it was bought by Mr Jack Taylor in 1939 and converted into a motor repair business.

## Barbers
In the early part of the 20th century, ladies in the village either did their own hair or had to go to Bedford. There is no record of a ladies' hairdresser. Men could go to Ernest Porter (Rardy) who lived at 11 Gold Street and cut hair at the small building just behind 58 High Street. Mrs Eva Pentlow from the blacksmith's at 62 High Street and Mrs Joan Crowsley at 13 Gold Street also cut hair in their own homes. In the 1970s a hairdressing salon was opened in the office premises of Taylor's Garage where Litchfield is now, but it did not remain there for long.

## Blacksmiths, Garages and Agricultural Engineers
At the turn of 1900 the village smithy was at its present location but the forge was a thatched building on the right side of the frontage of the present house at 62 High Street. It was run at that time by William Wyant. Mr Alfie Pentlow came from Dean to work at the blacksmiths.

*Bob Pentlow and horses waiting to be shod*

Alfie Pentlow bought the business in 1917 and built it up into a thriving concern. His son, Edward (Ted), took over from him and his grandson Robert runs the business today. The blacksmiths was also the site of the first motor cycle business with petrol pumps.

Mr Jack Taylor ran the motor cycle and petrol business and later moved to the site of Kings, the bakers, now Litchfield. It became a large motor garage with forecourt, pumps and a large workshop. Mr Jack Taylor ran the business with his son, Clive. The business closed in early 1979 and a firm Royale Racing moved in to manufacture racing cars. When Royale Racing moved out the garage remained empty for some years before becoming the Litchfield housing development.

WJH Motors took over the site that had been the Bedford Rural District Council depot for the dustcarts at the northern end of the village, next to the bridge over the brook. Keysonian coaches had used the site for a couple of years and John Hodgson opened WJH Motors there in 1968. He had petrol pumps installed and uses the workshop for car repairs and MOT testing. In the early days, Ruth Clark remembers delivering paraffin on Friday afternoons, to village households who still used paraffin heaters. The business now has a new car franchise and provides employment for ten people from Riseley and the surrounding area. Many young men from the village have also benefited from the opportunity to serve an apprenticeship in the workshop.

In addition to the blacksmiths there was an agricultural engineering workshop on the site of the new houses next to Laburnum House, opposite Church Lane. This was run by the Hewin family. In addition to repair and maintenance work on agricultural machinery and steam engines, Mr Hewin also manufactured agricultural equipment. Some of his equipment is still to be found in museums. The business was taken over by John Baines.

## Carpenters and Wheelwrights

This trade gave the village one of its most known local families and characters, the Litchfields.

In 1900 the business was run by Jesse Litchfield. He passed the business on to his son Eli who in turn passed it to his son Stanley. Stanley Litchfield ran it until his retirement. The workshop was a wooden building on the site of the new police post next to 35 High Street.

*Ted Pentlow on his motorcycle in front of the Petrol Pumps*

All types of carpentry and wheelwrighting were carried out. The Litchfields were also the village coffin makers and undertakers.

Inside the workshop was the pit where wheels would be built. The hub was laid across the pit and the wooden spokes driven into the sockets cut into the hub. As more spokes were built up, the lower ones would point downwards into the pit, enabling the hub to stay at floor level for comfortable working.

The finished wheel was then taken across the road to the sawing pit where the steel tyres were fitted. The steel tyres were heated in a fire built from shavings and sawdust. Many tyres would be heated at one time, all stacked in a conical heap with the largest at the bottom. When hot enough, the tyres were lifted from the fire with long tongs, and lowered into position around the outside of the newly made wheel. Water was poured over the rim to cool and shrink it, making a good tight fit.

*Eli Litchfield with a wheel he had made*

Other carpenters in the village included William Dennis, William Farrar and Fred Knight (Wheelwright).

**Lace Making**
The making of pillow lace was a very important cottage industry in Riseley. Pillow lace developed in two main areas of England, Honiton in Devon and in the East Midland counties of Bedfordshire, Buckinghamshire and Northamptonshire. Mainly women and girls were employed. They could supplement their household incomes working from their homes, earning as much as 8d to 10d (4p) a day.

Lacemakers in Riseley could have either traded their lace to local shopkeepers such as Mrs Savage or via Toamiss Campion who dealt with Braggins of Bedford. Thomas Lester was a famous lace manufacturer in Bedford and would have traded in Riseley lace.

As it was such an important supplement to incomes most villages had lace schools where children from as young as six or seven were taught to make lace. There was one such school in Riseley run by Annie Baker.

*Riseley lace school, circa 1910*

In the manufacture of the lace the young children could work four to five hours per day, the older children six to eight hours and the young women 12-15 hours.

Some public holidays were linked to lace making. Some areas celebrated Tanders (St Andrew's Day, 30 November) or Catterns (St Catherine's Day on 25 November). These were sometimes called Candle Day being the first day when lace had to be made using candle light.

*Betsy Fairey with her lace cushion and candle outside her home at Whitegates*

Betsy Fairey was a Riseley lace maker. In poor light lace makers used a glass globe filled with water which would magnify and concentrate the light of a candle on to the lace cushion.

Riseley celebrated Shrove Tuesday as a half-day holiday and a game played by local children on this day was *'Long Eche'*. An eche was the parchment which contained the lace pattern, two put together was a long eche. A scarf would represent the eche and two children would hold it whilst others ran underneath and try to avoid being caught.

The First World War saw the end of lace making in Riseley as industrial machinery took over from the homeworker.

## Earning a Living

**The Royal Aircraft Establishment**
The RAE dominated every day life in Riseley for many years. The low flying aircraft were a familiar sight and noise and many villagers found employment there.

When the USAAF 306th Bomb Group left Thurleigh airfield on 15 December 1945, the British Government saw potential in the site for use as a National Aeronautical Establishment (NAE).

The original plan was to link it with the wartime airfields at Little Staughton and Twinwoods to make one enormous facility with a five-mile long runway and a two-mile taxiway. Work was begun, but advances in technology meant that a runway of this length was no longer required and it was abandoned. The deep cutting on the road to Thurleigh, which would have been under the taxiway, is the only remaining evidence of the project.

However, between 1946 and 1957 the airfield at Thurleigh was expanded and one of the longest runways in Europe – 10,500 feet long and 300 feet wide – was constructed.

Until the closure of the RAE in March 1994, the skies around Riseley were busy with aircraft carrying out their various activities. Virtually every aircraft of the period has been based at or visited the airfield at sometime.

One of the most notable activities at the RAE was the Blind Landing Experimental Unit. This unit worked on systems to enable aircraft to land in fog and bad weather. How many passengers on modern jets realise that landings in bad weather would not be possible without the work done in the 1960s in the skies over Riseley?

An amusing tale is told relating to the first flight from Thurleigh of the Blackburn NA39 Buccaneer Carrier Based Jet on 30 April 1958. It came up Riseley High Street so low that all the overhead telephone and electricity wires came down! This is a true story, but the plane was on the back of a lorry at the time, being brought by road to be prepared for its first flight on the RAE's long runway.

In the 1960s and 1970s British Airways' pilots trained in Boeing 707, VC 10 and Boeing 747 jumbo jets. They practised *'circuits and bumps'* almost every weekday evening – sometimes until 10.30 at night.

At the height of the Cold War the Vulcan 'V' bombers came to Thurleigh airfield for an annual exercise. The aircraft were fully loaded with nuclear weapons and based at the Keysoe end of the airfield. The idea was for them to practise operating away from their home base. What a sight and sound their scramble take off over the village was!

John Gell and Pete Holowell were on the V bomber base with their council tanker lorry when it was caught in a mock Soviet attack. They were informed that they had been killed in the incident – is John Gell the only Riseley resident to become a victim of a nuclear onslaught?

On Friday 30 January 1981, the SAS mounted an anti-terrorist hi-jacking exercise, using a VC10 parked at the Riseley end of the airfield. All radio and TV was blacked out for most of the evening. Villagers were in the dark about what was happening and had to wait until after the weekend for an explanation.

The RAE site is now used for storage of vehicles and for motor sport hospitality by Bedford Autodrome.

**The Chapel Gallery** – Charlotte Phelps
The Moravian Chapel has been used as a gallery and picture framing workshop since 1977. When it was purchased by its present owners in 1975 it was in a sorry state. All the windows were damaged or bricked up and there was nothing remaining of the panelled interior, pulpit and hand pumped organ. There was a crude staging along the north and south internal walls – installed to create extra floor space.

The possibility of the building becoming a gallery was obvious: excellent natural light and plenty of height, floor and wall space. The front doors were replaced, in keeping with the originals, the interior painted white and modern spotlighting installed. Part of the interior is now partitioned off as a framing workshop, which over the years has handled the framing of thousands of pictures and other items such as, on one occasion, an owl!

Earning a Living

The gallery area offers space to artists – local and otherwise – who wish to display their work. An ongoing programme of special exhibitions features the work of well-known contemporary artists from the Bedford area as well as others from further afield.

**Brook House** – Helen Constant
The largest house in the village today must be Brook House. It has evolved over the centuries from a cottage dwelling for a family to a residential home for 20 people.

The original cottage built in the 17th century was large for its time. It was *'a timber framed range partly on a stone plinth cased in brick'*. Parts of the wattle and daub walls have been preserved although much has been destroyed over the years and none of the original rough case colour wash remains. The roof was of handmade clay tiles, probably locally made, and evidence of workmanship seems to prove it was tiled by a bricklayer not a roof tiler. But the colony of long eared bats that have lived happily in the roof for many years do not seem to object.

During the 18th century the first extension, a small wing made from Riseley brick was built on the back.

The first big change came 100 years later and altered the whole appearance of the building; it now looked

*Brook House in 1986*

153

like a grand Victorian house. A large double-bay frontage was added by Philip Humbly Banks. He was an important man in North Bedfordshire being the Bedford Registrar and Coroner, and Medical Officer for Bedford and Riseley Union. These were the workhouses – Bedford's being the now North Wing Hospital and Riseley's the humbler one situated on Rotten Row, now cottages, numbers 14 and 16.

The next century brought many changes of owners and occupants. The family living there at the turn of the century left following Mr Green's death in the flu epidemic of 1919. Before many years had passed Riseley's most famous visitor, Edward, Prince of Wales, made use of the Measures' livery stables for his horses, when he took part in the point to point races.

By war time the house was split into several flats and many of today's Riseley residents lived there for a time. It continued being rented until it was bought in 1986 by Helen and Bryan Constant and Barbara and Colin Jones, with plans to turn it into a residential home for the elderly.

By then it was in a very run down state. Any renovation had to meet the strict rules laid down by officialdom, so it was a challenge to restore what was by now a Grade 2 listed building sympathetically and keep the inspectors happy. But it was achieved and Brook House Residential Home opened in June 1987. It had two big lounges, 11 bedrooms, a vast kitchen, a cellar now a modernised laundry room and one resident! Numbers grew quickly and before long it was filled with residents and brought employment to 25 people, most of whom came from Riseley and worked part time.

But change was not over. Under new Social Service rulings it became clear that to survive, Brook House had to change again. Another wing was built and the existing one extended to match. The old stable and coach house was converted into a day centre to cater for the increasing need for care in the community. The centre provides support and a break for those in need and their carers. So Brook House is now the biggest employer in the village, employing 35 staff, ranging from full time care assistants to teenagers who befriend the residents and help in

Earning a Living

the serving of meals. Most of the staff have worked there for many years and some from first opening.

*Brook House restored and extended, October 1999*

Each century has brought its alterations to the building, all reflecting the diversity of daily life within its changing walls.

**Instrument Engineering** – Christine Futter
The engineering company known as Instrument Engineering was brought to Riseley in 1972, by Keith and Christine Futter. The business took over the old wooden workshop previously used by Mr Stanley Litchfield – and Stanley's father Eli, before him.

Currently occupying the purpose built workshop at the foot of Keysoe Road, Instrument Engineering is a family owned engineering manufacturing concern specialising in the design, manufacture and development of a range of specialist welding equipment designed to weld together high value, high quality components used in the engineering industry.

Typical applications of Instrument Engineering products include welding the housings of temperature sensing thermocouples used in aircraft engines built by most of the world's major jet engine manufacturers.

155

*Instrument Engineering*

Other uses include welding stainless steel wire mesh filter elements used in ultra – high purity filters for the chemical industry, hydraulic control lines on aircraft landing gear, and chemical process plant.

Customers delight in coming to Riseley to discuss projects at the Keysoe Road Works, frequently having driven from far flung parts of the UK and occasionally arriving from the USA, Norway, Turkey and Australia.

# In Times of War
**Peter Smith**

Riseley has been witness to much conflict in the early centuries due to the invasion of these islands. This has been covered in "A Clearing in the Brushwood", so we can move to the 14th century when there started a long series of wars, truces and periods of peace between England and France known collectively as the Hundred Years War. The fighting took place in France with three major battles, Crecy in 1346, Poitiers in 1356 and Agincourt in 1415.

The principal weapon of the English army at that time was the longbow. Peculiar to the English (the French favoured the crossbow), the longbow was some six feet in length and the bowmen preferred their bows to be made from yew, although elm and beech were also used to prevent the total destruction of yew trees. Churchyards all over England still have yew trees in them, which were planted to provide wood for bows. The arrows, three feet long, were capable of penetrating armour at 250 yards.

The English archer of the Hundred Years War was a true professional fighting man. Such was its success, that Edward III conferred honour on the longbow and archery practice became compulsory throughout the land.

*Archers at the butts*

Although records have not survived for that time it is almost certain that the young men of Riseley would have practised their skills at the village butts. These were located at the end of Rotten Row where there is now just a country lane called The Butts. It is not hard to imagine lines of archers firing their arrows probably towards what is now Lodge Farm.

**Muster Lists**

*RYSELEY*
*Archers*
Thomas Bankes
Edward Polton
Robert Watson
William Barford
Gabriell Shaller
*Byllmen*
Thomas Payn
Ede Fox
Thomas Browne
John Storer
Robert Dawes
William Woodward
John Woodward
John Lawrence sen.
Edward Nicolles
John Parysshe
Richard Rede
*Harnoys*
Robert Sakvyle:
 Thomas Hatley:
 Robert Bankes to harnoys a man
The towneship besides theym to harnoys a man
*Summa of Archers v*
*Summa of Byllmen xj*
*Summa of Harnoys ij*

*Riseley Muster List - 1539*

The obligation to provide men, weapons and equipment for local defence can be traced back to Anglo-Saxon times when able-bodied men were liable for military service. The Statute of Winchester of 1285 decreed the weapons that every man must keep according to his assessed wealth and ordered that inspections take place twice a year.

In 1558 this Statute was superseded by the *'Act of the Keeping of Arms and Horses'*. Men were assessed in groups, according to income. Those worth £5-£10 a year provided a coat of plated armour, a bill or halberd, longbow and steel helmet; those worth £1,000 or more were obliged to provide 16 horses, 80 suits of armour, 40 pikes, 30 longbows, 20 bills and steel helmets.

The County forces were usually mustered together when there was a threat of foreign invasion or local unrest. The Bedfordshire lists are typical of the period and as the one for Riseley shows they continued to use the bow and bill.

The bill, a long handled weapon with a hooked blade, needed comparatively little skill in handling and bore a strong resemblance to the farm implement from which it originated.

# In Times of War

Muster lists continued through the reign of Elizabeth I when there was a threat of invasion from Catholic Spain, but by 1603 the danger had receded and it was in that year that the *'Act of Taking Musters'* was rescinded. There was, however, confusion over the nature of military obligations and in 1612 the Counties reverted to annual general musters.

By 1626 there was a growing dispute between the Crown and the Counties over the control of the Militia and this foreshadowed one of the major issues in the Civil War.

In 1644 Parliament had gained the upper hand with the Royalists defeated; Cromwell's new Model Army was formed. With the restoration of the Monarchy in 1660 new Militia Acts were passed to strengthen the authority of the Crown and to face the threat of rebellion. Bedfordshire raised 120 horses and 456 men of which Riseley provided five men equipped with muskets and two with corslets (body armour).

## National Defence Volunteers

The Defence of the Realm Act of 1803 was intended to create reserves of men not already serving in the military and materials. With Napoleon Bonaparte threatening invasion, lists were drawn up of men to evacuate the civil population and adopt a scorched earth policy to deprive the invaders of food, whilst ensuring the defenders were properly supplied. Surviving records show that Riseley provided men and

### RISELY

| Persons having teams | Waggons | Carts | Horses | Drivers |
|---|---|---|---|---|
| Willm. Hills | 1 | 1 | 8 | 2 |
| Thos. Gell | 2 | | 8 | 2 |
| Wm. Hart | 1 | | 5 | 1 |
| Mrs George | 1 | | 4 | 1 |
| Mr Robins | | 1 | 2 | 1 |
| Wm. Rootham | | 2 | 4 | 2 |
| Jos. Rootham | 1 | | 3 | 1 |
| Wm Burbidge | 1 | | 3 | 1 |
| Jabez Eldred | | 1 | 3 | 1 |
| Jos Wilkinson | 1 | | 4 | 1 |
| Edwd. Eyles | | 1 | 1 | 1 |
| Saml. Pool | | 1 | 3 | 1 |
| John Sharman | | 1 | 2 | 1 |
| Jos Farrer | | 1 | 2 | 1 |
| Thos. Rootham | | 1 | 3 | 1 |
| John Rootham | | | | |
| Wm. Bonfield | | 1 | 1 | 1 |
| Philip Dickens | | 1 | 1 | 1 |
| Wm Lormon | | 1 | 1 | 1 |
| George Porter | | 1 | 1 | 1 |
| Thomas Hull | | 1 | 1 | 1 |
| Mr Smith | | 1 | 1 | 1 |
| Total | 8 | 16 | 61 | 24 |

| Millers and Bakers | Flour and Bread per week |
|---|---|
| Edwd. Eyles. Baker | 10 sacks |
| Saml. Pool. Miller | 10 loads |
| John Sharman Baker | 8 sacks |
| Thomas Hull Baker | 10 sacks |

Total 1 Miller 3 Bakers.
    Miller 10 additional loads.  Bakers 28 sacks
Jos. Morton, Vicar

*National Defence List for Riseley*

materials as shown. The Riseley village vicar in 1803, the Revd William Braithwaite reported that, *'the able-bodied men of the Parish liable for service against a possible French invasion volunteered to a man and gave three cheers'.*

*A Bedfordshire Militia Man - 1803*

One Riseley villager in particular deserves mention here. In 1801 William Boddington married Mary Odell and in 1803 a daughter Elizabeth was born. The parish records show that in 1805 Mary and child were removed from the parish and returned to Mary's original parish of Titchmarsh in Northamptonshire. The reason was that William had joined the Bedfordshire Militia along with two other villagers, John Barker and William Hart.

In 1805 the Duke of Somersetshire came with his Regiment – the 40th Foot to Bedford. The three men enlisted in the 1st Battalion of that Regiment, were paid the princely sum of £1 10s 0d (£1.50) for 30 days and then marched to Bristol where they embarked for South America. From there the Regiment was involved in the Peninsula War in 1813 where William was promoted to corporal being paid 11d (4$^1$/$_2$p) per day. He was subsequently wounded at Pampeluna, Spain.

In 1815 William and his Regiment were at Waterloo where the Allies, under Wellington, finally defeated Napoleon. After his return to England, he was awarded the Waterloo Medal as all ranks were. The Regiment was then sent to Scotland in 1817 and reduced in size. Because of this, and his wounds, he was discharged at Chelsea on a pension of 6d (2½p) a day.

He had been away from the village for nearly 14 years. There is no record of him returning to Riseley – presumably he returned to his wife and child in Northamptonshire.

After Waterloo, the militia in Bedfordshire was generally used, in the last resort, to aid civil power during unrest or riots. After the Napoleonic Wars there had been sporadic agricultural unrest in Bedfordshire which became more serious in 1828-29 and culminated in the *'Swing riots'* of 1836. In 1832 Riseley farmworkers were among those who agitated for a wage rise and the constable in the village became the target for attacks.

The Militia Act of 1806 had been passed with the aim of training men who were eligible. Clergymen, schoolmasters and medical men were exempt from service. Apprentices and poor men with more than one child, were also exempt but were still liable for training. Quakers and United Brethren escaped the provisions of the Act on payment of a fine of between £1 and £7.

Many Riseley men enrolled in the militia, men like James Croot and William Chamberlain whose descendants were to take part in future wars.

In 1828-29 serious cases of arson and poaching in the county encouraged magistrates to rely on locally enrolled special constables to keep the peace rather than the militia. This marked a significant shift in policy and the formation of the Bedfordshire Police Force in 1840 ensured that the role of the militia as an internal peacekeeping force was over.

Later in the 19th century it was the regular army that met the demands of the Crimean and Boer wars and one man we can mention here is Wilfred Ashworth, grandfather of John Ashworth who kindly wrote the foreword for this book. Wilfred served in India, China and the Boer War in South Africa. On leaving the army, Wilfred's Colonel – Colonel Jackson – bought The Mallowry and Wilfred became the estate manager. Another Boer War participant was 'Clary' Bateman who won the Military Medal.

*Wilfred Ashworth*

*'Clary' Bateman*

During World War One Wilfred was recalled to the army and served in the prisoner of war camp at Kimbolton.

## World War One

Sometimes called *'the Great War'* and *'the war to end all wars'*, the war of 1914-18 revived the same spirit of patriotism that had typified the response in Napoleonic times. At the start, conscription was unnecessary, as men throughout the country volunteered in their hundreds of thousands. Riseley played its part and many men enlisted at the various local recruiting centres. Most joined the army, and to be together, most Riseley men joined the Bedfordshire Regiment. Some, however, joined the Navy and James Valentine was an air mechanic with the Flying Corps, which later became the RAF.

Beryl Wallis' father, Aubrey Savage, had tried unsuccessfully to join the RAF at the tender age of 17, with his friend Stanley Litchfield. He was however accepted by the Royal Marine Light Artillery. As he recorded in his diary, *'I received the King's shilling in the form of a two shilling piece which covered myself and a pal of mine'*.

*Aubrey Savage*     *John George Rootham*

As the war dragged on many serving men were mentioned in the local newspapers. Dr and Mrs Collins' son, Captain Arthur Collins won the Military Cross. Corporal Samuel Barker was awarded the Military Medal and Captain Arthurs, whose grandfather had fought at Waterloo, was mentioned in despatches.

Albert Sharman remembers one villager who had joined up. *'Harry Brown, he was shot in the head, but the bullet passed right through and killed the man next to him. Harry survived and returned to the village.'*

Within the village the war had its effect too. Prices of everyday goods rose steeply and as the Bedfordshire Times reported shortly before Christmas 1914, *'Owing to the high price of all goods due to the war, the bakers of Riseley find it impossible to give their usual Christmas boxes this year'*.

Farms in the village had a labour shortage and local girls were employed for farm work. These subsequently became known as land girls. Margaret Waldock remembers that at Town Farm Carolyn (Carrie) Partridge and Beatrice Wildman worked throughout the war period, as did Poppy and Isobel Collins, daughters of the local doctor.

*Land girl Carolyn (Carrie) Partridge at Town Farm*

Kings Farm, as Albert Sharman recalls, became a night stopover for the many horses pulling gun carriages through the village.

Local organisations did their bit for the war effort by staging fund-raising events. A fund was set up at the school to purchase wool to knit socks for the Bedfordshire Regiment. The school log records that on 25 September 1917, *'The school was closed in the afternoon of each day to enable the children to pick blackberries for the Army and Navy'*.

And so with the ending of the war in 1918, the men started to come home. Of the 57 who went off to fight 17 did not return as the war memorial records. 'Tink' Hancock was unfortunate to have his toes shot off and, on his return, got around the village on a donkey and cart.

*'Tink' Hancock and donkey cart*

In Times of War

*Armistice Day, Riseley*

*Children celebrating the Armistice on Gold Street bridge*

Of those inscribed on the war memorial there are names that have been in the village for centuries and this is especially true of Wildman, Gell, Hancock, Croot and Sawford.

On 5 May 1920 a commemorative service was held at the church and the war memorial was dedicated.

There was now a period of peace that was to last 21 years. A whole generation of young men had been reduced by one third and now with the recovery, the next generation had just a relatively short time before the next conflict.

**World War Two**
In the late 1930s there was general unease at the ranting and raving of Adolf Hitler and the ambitions of a revitalised Germany. When Prime Minister Chamberlain spoke of *'Peace in our time'* there was some relief within the country, but to many there was a foreboding of another war. So it proved, and as Germany invaded Poland, Britain and France declared war on Germany on 3 September 1939.

It was not surprising that there was no general rush to the recruiting stations. Most people had memories of the shocking slaughter of the First World War. However, an army was sent to France made up of the regular army and the Territorials. In Riseley, four men from the village had joined the

*'Steve' Stevens and Leslie Hawkins*

Territorial Army prior to the outbreak of war – Jack Hancock, Gilbert Barker, Leslie Hawkins and Horace (Steve) Stevens. Consequently they were the *'first to go'* – more of them later.

Aubrey Savage who had served in World War One had been retained in the Royal Fleet Reserve and so he, too, was recalled early. He served on HMS Velox and was involved in convoy duties in the North Atlantic, which was very hazardous with Germany's U-boats attempting to cut Britain's lifeline to the rest of the world.

**Evacuees**
At the outbreak of war the Government was worried about the bombing of Britain's cities. The wheels were set in motion to evacuate children, especially from London.

Bedfordshire received some 36,000 and Riseley became host to 94 children from North London. They actually arrived two days before war broke out and were accompanied by their teachers. They were assembled in the village and allotted to villagers who had the capacity in their homes to take them. As Betty Cerasale recalls: *'I remember them arriving and they were billeted all round the village. We had two girls with us. They were from Burleigh Girls' school, we used to call them "the Burleigh bug squashers!" But they fitted in well here and at the school and, of course, after the war they went home.'*

With the new arrivals, the school became overcrowded, so the policy of bussing in children from other villages was stopped. There was a temporary air raid shelter within the school and all children were issued with gas masks. Mr Ashworth was the chief *'gas mask man'* and everyone went to him to replace broken masks. Further evacuees arrived from Sussex accompanied by Mr Apps who was to become very involved with fund-raising events for the war effort.

In late May 1940 with France close to capitulation, a sizeable proportion of the British army was evacuated from Dunkirk. Jack Hancock had been sent to France with the British Expeditionary Force and in his own words: *'At Dunkirk we were unable to get away, so some of us made our way further down the coast. We met up with some French troops and a French officer pulled his pistol on us – he thought we were deserters!*

*We eventually picked up a Belgian fishing boat and got to Southampton. We sat about – nobody seemed to know what to do with us and we ended up in Ross-on-Wye. It was a day and a half before we even had a cup of tea.'*

Ida Hancock (now Ida Bates) used to cycle to Sharnbrook station to catch the train to her work in Bedford. One day she recalls, *'A train came into Sharnbrook packed with soldiers from Dunkirk. They were in a terrible state and they were leaning out of the windows asking if we were going to Bedford. They passed notes to us so that we could let their families know that they were all right. I felt so sorry for them and we delivered the scraps of paper.'*

**'We shall defend our Island'** – Winston Churchill, June 1940
With the threat of invasion, local Home Guard units were formed and in Riseley amongst the many who enlisted in *'Dad's Army'* as it became known, were J Felce, W Hancock, C Harris, J Howard, C Pole, J K and G Rootham, A Savage and H Waldock.

With weapons in short supply, the men drilled with broomsticks, although, as Tony Cerasale remembers, *'Henry Waldock was one of the heads of the unit as he had a .22 rifle he used for rabbiting'*. Later on they all got rifles and used to practise every Sunday morning in the sandpit.

As with the rest of the country, Riseley observed a strict blackout, and it was the responsibility of the Air Raid Warden to enforce it. Jock Westley, Albert Sharman and Fred Gell were members of the Air Raid Precaution Unit. Both Gordon Vincent and Tony Cerasale remember Jock Westley riding down the High Street on his horse, blowing his whistle and shouting *'Air Raid!'*, although apparently the horse would not go past The Fox and Hounds until he and Jock had had a glass of beer!

In fact, a stick of bombs did land on the Keysoe Road and as Tony Cerasale again remembers: *'several of the bombs failed to explode so they were taken down to The Five Bells where everyone came to have a look!'* Some air raid shelters were provided in the village but seldom used. John Gell recalls: *'We had one but never used it – it was full of hens!'*

# In Times of War

An auxiliary Fire Service was also formed with Albert Sharman, Bernard Hancock, 'Crom' Hancock, Arthur Sawford and Mr Apps amongst its members. They used an old Humber car with a trailer pump and pumped water direct from the brook.

## 'Eyes and Ears'

The Observer Corps had been formed in 1925 and was the *'Eyes and Ears of the RAF'*. Their task was to provide information on all aircraft flying over the UK. The Riseley Post was opened in 1937 close to the windmill in Mill Lane (now the Keysoe Road). Members were recruited locally. Ralph Savage and Jack Taylor were the first appointees, but as war loomed other villagers joined them: Horace Felce, Ted Pentlow, Les Vincent, Jock Westley, Jim Felce and others. Later, as the post became busier, women were encouraged to join. Ida Hancock, Sue Bates, Anna Moore and Rosemary Prince all served as observers.

*Royal Observer Corps Post, Riseley*
*Left to Right: Back Row: Ted Pentlow, Godfrey Sealey, Jim Ellis, Percy Hopkins*
*Front Row: Ida Hancock, 'Cub' Westley*

The post, code-named *'Roger One'*, consisted of a wooden hut with bunks and a coke stove (a cup of tea and a fry-up always welcome), a raised platform with a chart table and sighting equipment to plot an aircraft's position and height. Binoculars were provided as well as a field telephone connected to an operations room.

All aircraft had to be plotted whether enemy or friendly. The area around Riseley was very busy with American B-17s, RAF pathfinder Mosquitos from Little Staughton as well as enemy bombers passing over to attack the industrial Midlands.

The post was manned 24 hours a day and divided into two men (or women) watches. Ida Hancock and Anna Moore were on duty one wild and windy evening when as Ida remembers, *'It was spooky enough with the wind and the windmill creaking when we got a call on the field telephone. We were warned that a POW had killed his guard and was on the loose. We were terrified, so we got the old rifle that was kept at the post but we had a job lifting it, let alone firing it!'* The POW who was armed with a rifle and ammunition he had taken from the guard was finally caught at a farm near Pertenhall, where, after an exchange of fire with the farmer, he was shot and killed.

On a different occasion, Ida came on duty with another girl. *'We brewed up as usual and we made several cups of tea on that watch. We thought the tea tasted somewhat unusual until we looked in the kettle and there was a dead mouse in it which the previous watch had kindly left us!'*

Observers were paid the princely sum of 1s 3d an hour (6$^1$/$_2$p) but Horace Felce and Ida remember their time at the post as being friendly, interesting and with a spirit typical of those days.

In recognition of its contribution during the Battle of Britain the corps became The Royal Observer Corps and continued until the end of the war and beyond.

**Village at War**
As the war progressed there was a shortage of fuel and food rationing was introduced. People were encouraged to grow their own food. *'Dig for Victory'* was the slogan of the time. What is now Ross Meadow became a series of allotments that to a lesser degree still exist today.

The people of the village played their part in the war effort. Every week there was some kind of fund-raising event – a dance, whist-drive or show by the theatre group. The proceeds went to the Red Cross, the Comfort Fund, Allied prisoners of war and on one particular occasion £5 10s (£5.50) was the contribution to the Spitfire Fund. Also, as the Bedfordshire Times reported: *'26 members of HM forces from Riseley each received £1. Mrs Taylor of the WVS supplied wool for knitting balaclavas, mittens, scarves and other items for the men serving.'* One such helper was Betty Cerasale whose mother got her to knit a scarf. She remembers, *'It turned out far too large, but I put my name in it – but I never heard from the recipient'*. Pearl Felce was helping by making and selling children's toys.

As in the first war, extra farm labour was needed and once again the land girls came into their own. They were billeted in hostels around the area and were brought in to work on the farms. Among these were Mary Wallis and Lily Felce. Mary says, *'We were paid 48 shillings a week (£2.40) but 24 shillings went towards our board and keep'*.

Mary and Lily both remember that the work was hard, involving a variety of tasks – ploughing, harrowing, rolling, ditch digging, manure spreading, threshing and haymaking to name but a few.

*Lily Felce*

*Mary Wallis*

News came in of the men serving in the forces. In 1942 Mrs Barker of 111 High Street, was informed by the War Office that her son Gilbert was missing. It was not until April 1943 that she heard that he was a POW. Gilbert had been sent to Singapore and was captured by the Japanese. For the next three and a half years he worked with thousands of others on the Burma-Thailand railway. Gilbert was lucky to survive, as many died on that infamous railway.

Leslie Hawkins was involved with the construction of portable Mulberry Harbours used with such effect to maintain supplies on the Normandy beaches on D-Day.

'Steve' Stevens was posted to a most unenviable unit – bomb disposal! After a period of duty in Hull dealing with unexploded German bombs, he was sent to the Middle East on similar dangerous work.

**POWs**
As the war slowly turned in the Allies' favour, prisoners of war started to appear in the area. They were billeted locally and were put to work on the farms. They were distinguished by having a yellow circle on the back of their working clothes. Italian POWs were the first to arrive after the Eighth Army's success in North Africa.

People who were in the village at that time remember them as being friendly and generally no trouble. Ellen Di Folco remembers them well. *'My mother-in-law would make pasta for them and they would make beautiful wicker baskets, rings and cigarette cases, and when my husband Joe lost a couple of front teeth they made him some false ones out of perspex.'*

Later the first German POWs began to arrive and they too, went to work on the farms. Harold Wallis remembers them as being hard working and he often used to take them back to their camp after work in his lorry. He says, *'Taking them back once, the fan belt broke and I had my head under the bonnet – they could have done anything, but they didn't, in fact they managed to make a temporary one out of string. We did have one with us who was a proper Nazi. One day he had finished his normal work so I put him to work on our garden, when I came back he had shaped the flower beds in the shape of a swastika!'*

Beryl Wallis, at that time living at High Barn Farm remembers one particular German POW, Johanne Hessling, who was a farmer in Germany before the war. Johanne used to cycle from the POW camp at Colmworth every day and, of course, being an ex-farmer was very useful to the farm. After the war Johanne returned home but kept in touch with Beryl's family and still does today.

The Germans too, were adept at making useful items especially children's toys. Phillip Nicholls had many made for him by Raimund Schlindwein. Raimund was 18 years old when captured and worked at Sackville Farm. After the war he married a local girl and still lives in Ravensden.

At Park Farm, John Ashworth also had fond memories of the Germans. One, named Fritz, was a special friend who gave him his Afrika Korps badge and taught him some German. Fritz came from Hamburg and John can remember him being consoled when news came of the devastating allied bombing of that city.

During their time in the village the enemy POWs were certainly not unwelcome, in fact they became part of village life at that time. This was also true of the next set of *'visitors'* to the community.

**Over Here**
In December 1941 the USA entered the war, and it was not long before American servicemen started to arrive in this country. Thurleigh airfield had initially been used by the Polish Air Force, but in September 1942 it became host to the 306th Bombardment Group of the US Air Force. This comprised four squadrons of B-17s popularly known as *'Flying Fortresses'*. Their first bombing mission was on the 9 October 1942 and in January 1943 they became the first American group to bomb Germany.

American support units were also stationed around Riseley and Melchbourne Park. With their arrival, village life changed significantly. Betty Cerasale and several other villagers remember the High Street having one continuous convoy of vehicles carrying bombs. *'It took ages to cross the road,'* Betty recalls, *'but we didn't mind because the Americans were very friendly and would throw sweets and gum to us kids.'*

*B-17 'Eager Beaver' and personnel*

Bombs were stacked all around the village – along the Sharnbrook road, Pippin Wood and the road to Sackville Farm. Albert Sharman says, '*All my farm land was up and around the Sharnbrook road and there were thousands of bombs up there – the Americans had a guard post there and I used to have a pass to get through*'.

*Bomb stack in Pippin Wood*

Harry Walker also needed a pass. *'I used to cycle to Harings Farm where I worked,'* says Harry. *'One day I had a mate with me who didn't have a pass, so we decided to go via The Butts, but the guard spotted us and started firing, we dived into a ditch with bullets pinging all around!'*

Tony Cerasale also had a narrow escape. *'I was up near the airfield working and it was just getting dark, when one of the Yanks got into a parked aircraft and then into the top gunner's turret and let a burst of tracer bullets go – I was only 50 yards away!'*

With four squadrons at the airfield, life became quite noisy in the village. The US aircraft were involved in daylight bombing raids.

They would take off in the early morning and circle, waiting for other aircraft from neighbouring stations to join up into formation, and then proceed on their mission. The sky was one mass of planes, recalls Gordon Vincent. *'Us kids would watch and wait for their return. They would fire red Very flares if they had any wounded on board. We kids spent a lot of time up at the airfield, and the Yanks would let us carry the ammunition to the test range. We had quite a collection of live bullets and we would take the heads off and collect the cordite, but the police got to hear of it and confiscated the lot.'*

In a time of shortage and rationing the Americans seemed to have everything – everything that is, except fresh eggs. Gordon Vincent and John Gell both tell of collecting eggs and swapping them for gum and sweets. John Ashworth had his own way of egg delivery as he remembers: *'The airfield perimeter was surrounded by barbed wire and was patrolled by MPs with dogs. Foxes had made little runs under the wire, so I would pop an egg in my mouth and crawl under. I was surprised by a patrol once and inadvertently bit on the egg – I've hated raw egg ever since!'*

Park Farm where John lived was close to a dispersal point for aircraft with a Nissen hut that the aircrew used. *'I was sort of adopted by the crew and they would let me sit in the aircraft and one day smuggled me aboard for a test flight.'*

After the aircraft had taken off in the mornings, the ground crews would wander down to the village. The White Horse pub was a particular

Riseley – Our Village

favourite of theirs and Aubrey Felce, who as a boy living there, remembers the fun of the pub being full. They would stay until the aircraft began returning and then start walking up Lowsdon Lane.

*B-17s returning after their 200th mission*

All the local pubs were full at that time, as was the old village hall on Saturday nights. Betty Cerasale remembers the dances there. *'We usually had a dance on Saturday, but when the Americans came and sometimes brought their own band, it was lovely, much better than dancing to our old record-player.'*

Ida Hancock remembers the hall being packed, but also remembers those aircrews that were not there one week – one knew that they were missing from a raid. Ellen Di Folco's husband, Joe, used to play the piano in The Royal Oak for the Americans as well as the locals. Ellen recalls how sad it was when familiar faces no longer came down.

On Thursday 14 October 1943, there was nearly a wartime disaster. Jack Felce was working in the fields near Dean turn when a crippled B-17 Flying Fortress flew over at tree top height and crashed at the bottom end of the village. In fact it narrowly missed 170 High Street, crashing in the back garden and hitting a huge oak tree. A wing was torn off by the tree and the fuselage split in two. The pieces of the plane ended up in the old brickyard.

Fred Gell from 170 and Florrie Short from 166 rushed to the crash site expecting to find the crew all dead. There was blood in the wrecked fuselage, but the plane was empty.

*The crashed B-17 in the old brickyard*

The next day the USAAF official photographer visited the wreck and members of the crew visited to collect their belongings.

Research after the war revealed that the aircraft was Boeing B-17 Flying Fortress 42 5482 – *'Cat o' Nine Tails'* of the 303rd Bomb Group, Molesworth.

On that day it had joined 290 other B-17s on the famous daylight raid on the Schweinfurt ball bearing works. The target was heavily defended and 60 aircraft were shot down. A further 50 of those that returned to England were so badly damaged that they never flew again.

The crew of the *'Cat o' Nine Tails'* knew that their plane was too badly damaged to land. When they were safely over England they baled out, leaving the aircraft to fly on until it ran out of fuel. In fact the plane crashed only 14 miles, as the crow flies, from its starting point at Molesworth.

The crew all survived the remainder of the war and some have returned to Riseley to visit 170 High Street and see the crash site and the oak tree, which still bears the scars.

*American Servicemen in Riseley Church*

The Americans were especially kind to the children of the village. Gordon Vincent, John Gell and others all have fond memories of going to movies and concerts at either Thurleigh or Melchbourne. The highlight was the Christmas party when the Americans would send lorries to pick the children up. One particular Christmas, Ida Hancock had gone with some children to Thurleigh and during the party the Glenn Miller band was playing. Ida, who was known for her singing voice, joined the children in singing with the Miller band.

## In Times of War

**Victory**

After D-Day in 1944 it was only a matter of time before an Allied victory, but it was not until May 1945 that the war in Europe finally ended and in August that Japan surrendered. So another great war was concluded. The Americans departed and the serving men of the village began to come home. Forty seven had gone to serve with HM forces and all returned with the exception of Norman Harris who had died during flying training in Canada.

Victory and peace was celebrated throughout the country and Riseley rejoiced with VE (Victory in Europe) and VJ (Victory over Japan) parties. However, the shortages of food and fuel continued and many goods were *'on ration'* until the early '50s.

Military forces were maintained at wartime level and National Service was introduced. This was the time of the so-called *'Cold War'* when the USSR and the Western Allies faced each other across a divided Europe.

The Nuclear Age had dawned and the ROC post in Riseley which had *'stood down'* in 1945 was reopened in 1947 with a new role to play. They were part of a monitoring system to give alarm notice of the approach of radioactive fall-out. The post now became an underground reinforced concrete bunker, which could operate completely isolated with all services laid on.

*ROC Post 1967. Left to right: John Mead, 'Cub' Westley, Adrian Allan, Delia Smith, Gordon Vincent, Phillip Chambers, David Wilkinson*

179

Finally, with the Glasnost period and a general thawing of relations between East and West, the post closed in September 1991 as the Cold War concluded. British forces had joined with other United Nations in peacekeeping roles in places such as Korea, Malaya and Cyprus.

But, as we have seen in this chapter, wars affect all people whether in cities, towns or villages like our own. Let us hope that the generations that follow can enjoy a peace that those before them have fought so hard for.

*A Village named Riseley*
*Was off the map,*
*Then along came the war*
*That changed all that.*
*Evacuees came from London town*
*'Twas the government's idea*
*They would be safe and sound.*
*Some went to houses,*
*Some went to farms,*
*Some even slept outside in barns.*
*They did not fit in,*
*'Twas easy to see,*
*As their words had a different sound*

*Time went on and they settled down*
*And went to the village school,*
*But the shock that they got,*
*When they stood and took stock,*
*Was no lavatory chains to pull!*
*Only a burial plot, to bury their lot,*
*At the weekend after school*

*Then along came the Yanks*
*With their guns and their tanks*
*To woo the village belles.*
*The tales they told*
*Were hard to behold*
*When they went on their mission to hell.*
*As they took to the skies*
*There were tearful goodbyes,*
*So many never came back.*
*Now I'm happy to say*
*At the end of the day,*
*That Riseley is now on the map!*

**Ellen Di Folco**

# Hostelries and Public Houses
Andrew Gell

In common with most villages at the turn of the 1900s, Riseley was well provided with premises for the sale of beer and spirits. Many were beer houses rather than public houses – they did not have a bar and beer was brought through to the drinkers from the cellar and back room.

Most were not full time businesses. The landlords had other employment and just opened at certain times of the day or evenings only. Within living memory the public houses and beer houses in Riseley were as follows, listed from the top to the bottom end of the village.

The White Horse – opposite Lowsdon Lane
The Five Bells
The Boot – opposite Gold Street
The Red Lion – on the corner of Gold Street and Church Lane
The Fox and Hounds
The Swan – now The White House
The Royal Oak – now Oak House
The George and Dragon – now 2 Waldocks Close

The pubs and beer houses were a central part of village life and they were a source of entertainment as well as a venue for meetings for various village organisations.

The White Horse, which was a beer house with a six-day license, didn't open on Sundays. It used to host the annual club feast of the Riseley Tradesmen's Club. The event was recorded in June 1884 as being attended by 17 members who had a *'most excellent dinner'*. After dinner the members amused themselves by playing quoits and other games. Nuts were distributed during the afternoon to village children. The nuts were thrown into the air and the children had to scramble for them. Giving out nuts or sweets in this way seems to have been a tradition at several social events in the village. At the annual Moravian party held in the field where Paulsons Close is now, sweets were thrown to the children. Mrs Geary (nee Rootham) now aged 94 remembers the scramble for sweets and the thrill if you could pick up three or more!

*The White Horse*

The White Horse also hosted the teas for the cricket and the bowls teams. The bowling green was adjacent to The White Horse, although the only evidence remaining of it is the white lilac growing in the hedge alongside where the green used to be.

The Harvest Supper and Sale used to be held there before it was held in the old village hall. Before the First World War it was the venue for auctions of sections of woodland which villagers could coppice and clear, using the wood for fencing, in the garden and for cooking and heating. The small top branches of trees and undergrowth were bundled up and stacked to dry. The bundles were called *'faggots'* not to be confused with faggots that we buy from the butchers today to eat. When dry, the faggots were used for cooking in *'faggot ovens'* of which several still exist in the village. 76 High Street and 170 High Street still have them, although not in use. The faggots were burnt in the oven and when just embers remained and the oven was hot, the food would be put in to cook.

The sections of woodland auctioned were called *'ringes'*. It is said that one of the methods used at the auction was the pin stuck in the candle.

As the candle burnt down, the pin fell out. When the pin fell, the person having bid the highest amount was successful. Joseph Gell used to bid annually for *'ringes'* in Keysoe Park Wood.

The last landlord and landlady of The White Horse were Mr and Mrs Felce who moved in during 1944 and were there until it closed. Being the nearest pub to the wartime airfield at Thurleigh it was popular with the American airmen and Aubrey Felce can recall them often running out of beer at that time.

The meetings for one of the Friendly Societies connected with Riseley, The Odd Fellows, were held in The Five Bells. The other Friendly Society was the Ancient Order of Foresters and their regular meeting place was The Royal Oak. More on the Friendly Societies in "Sport, Parades and Village Events". The Five Bells was a Wells and Winch house before becoming part of the Greene King brewery.

In The Boot, the next pub down, the British Legion used to meet. Charlie Brooks, who was an amateur artist, painted large murals of county scenes on the walls in the meeting room there. Sadly, these no longer exist, but as he also painted pictures on a smaller scale, many of his paintings of houses in the village still do.

*The Five Bells*

*The Boot*

*The Red Lion*

There is no record of either The Red Lion or The Fox and Hounds being used for any social activities other than as pubs. As far as The Fox and Hounds is concerned this would have been because it was a small pub in its early days, with just a small lounge bar to the right of the entrance and a separate public bar on the left. The rest was barns and living accommodation – very different from what it is today. Robert Taylor, the famous bell founder, was born here as commemorated by the plaque over the fireplace.

*The Fox and Hounds, circa 1910*

The Swan was a beer house and has an unusual feature. The well is inside the premises, under the floor in the taproom. There was a metal cover for access. The Swan was a Wells and Winch house and was closed after the takeover by Greene King in the mid-1960s. It was only licensed to sell beer and tobacco. In its final days, John Gell recalls that for several nights it ran out of beer and the landlord took orders and then nipped down to The Royal Oak to fetch the beer!

The Royal Oak, at least the thatched part, is one of the older pubs in the village and within living memory has been a Charles Wells house. The main bar in the more recent brick built area was originally two rooms separated by a wooden sliding partition, which could be folded back to make one large room.

*The Swan*

*The Royal Oak with sheep in the street*

In addition to the regular meetings of the Ancient Order of Foresters, the local branch of the agricultural workers union, the National Association of Agricultural and Forestry Workers, held their meetings there. The agricultural workers union was well supported locally and for many years Mr Harry Brown was the local branch secretary.

The last pub in the village was The George and Dragon, which is now a private house at 2 Waldocks Close. It was a Paines of St Neots owned beer house and closed 1958-59. The last landlord was George Hopkins.

No mention has been made of the many darts, skittles and domino teams supported by the local pubs, as these would need a book to themselves.

*The George and Dragon – now 2 Waldocks Close*

## Did you know that . . .

*135 High Street is probably the oldest house in North Bedfordshire. It was constructed around the year 1480, originally as a one up one down dwelling. It is an ancient oak box framed house – an architectural style that does not quite fit with the local pattern. The stout oak frame, which is morticed and pegged, is in wonderfully original condition and retains much of its original wattle and daub infill.*

*The roof is double wind braced in each bay, whilst the tension bracing is uniquely rivetted through the vertical studwork, a fastening system normally associated with shipbuilding. This does not mean that it was constructed from re-used ships timbers, but local carpentry and heavy construction skills may have originated in the boatyards of St Neots.*

*An original four bar mullion window is in one of the lower bays and most other mullion windows have been fully or partially restored.*

*In 1722, the house received its first major renovation. The previously exposed timber frame was covered with lime plaster and the date was written on the front by the workman dragging his finger through the wet plaster – this remains.*

*Around 1990 a further extension was added, paying homage to the whimsical building regulations of the time. In this millennium year the house has finally been coated with fresh lime and ferrous sulphate, to restore it to its original splendour, ready for the next 1000 years!*

# Famous Faces
**Florence Wilkinson**

Riseley has been host to many famous people who have visited the village for a variety of reasons:

Hailie Selassi – King of Kings, Lion of Judah, Emperor of Abyssinia, spiritual leader of the Rastafarians – was the guest of Air Vice Marshall Slatter while he was living at the Mallowry.

Two princes from Siam went to a private school, which the Revd Dodds ran in the Old Vicarage in the 1920s. This was a language school and it is possible that other important people from abroad went there, but it is not known.

Mr Robertson – a partner in Robertson Engineering, Bedford – lived with his wife at Cobblestones. They entertained many well-known people including:

Randolph Churchill, son of the famous Winston Churchill; Aldo Ray, the film star; the Weston Brothers – a musical duo; Donald Swan of the TV and radio duo Flanders and Swan. He was amused that the pub opposite – The Swan – was his namesake and went over for a drink with the regulars.

Mary Churchill and her husband, Sir Nicholas Soames, MP for this constituency in the late 1950s and early 1960s, were entertained to lunch by Mrs Fitzgerald at 26 High Street.

Barbara Castle, Shirley Williams and David Blunkett, all government ministers at some time, have spoken at the village hall at the invitation of the North Bedfordshire Rural Labour Party. Ian Mikado also accompanied the then prospective parliamentary candidate to Riseley and spoke at the Margaret Beaufort School.

Carl Dane – the man who struck the gong at the beginning of the J Arthur Rank films put on a show in the old village hall. Locals were challenged to compete with him.

Doctor Hill, later Lord Hill, the Radio Doctor, came to Riseley to shoot at Town Farm during the time it was farmed by David Waldock.

David Barry who played Frankie Abbott in the very popular ITV comedy of the 1970s – the Fenn Street Gang – lived at 65 High Street for a while.

Noel Edmonds dropped in at The Fox and Hounds public house by helicopter in 1986.

A party of Saudi Arabians paid a visit to The Royal Observer Corps Post in Keysoe Road.

Pat Heslip, formerly Pat Davies, landlady at The Fox and Hounds from 1966 to 1976 recalls the visit of a famous pilot to fly some of the RAE research aircraft:

*'In the early 1970s we became the temporary "Home away from home" for the pilots and technicians of the Royal Navy Fleet Air Arm. They were from Plymouth and Yeovil, here to do all the tests on the ten new "Phantom" jet fighter planes. They were stationed at nearby RAE Thurleigh and were residing with us at The Fox and Hounds Inn. The Lounge Bar of The Fox and Hounds became an unofficial Clubhouse and meeting point for the Royal Aircraft Establishment personnel as well as the Royal Navy Party.*

*One lunchtime in the early summer of 1970, we had an official delegation ask us to provide dinner that evening for approximately a dozen RAE VIPs. It was impressed upon us that they wished to be alone in the dining room as a security precaution, and no comments were to be made regarding this booking – to this we assented.*

*So, the party of VIPs, both British and American – none of them in uniform – duly arrived, mostly dressed in sober lounge suits or sports jackets. They settled in quickly and quietly to a meal of fillet steak and trimmings or duck and orange sauce, followed by a choice of sherry trifle, blackberry and apple pie and cream and the cheese board.*

*It was a very serious and intense gathering and after coffee they resumed their discussion. One particular face seemed familiar, but puzzled me as to placing him. All became crystal clear when we were telephoned later by the RAE to explain why the secrecy and security was vital at the time.*

*Our guest of honour was none other than Neil Armstrong, the first man on the moon whose memorable words, "That's one small step for man, one great leap for mankind," will always be remembered – and he dined at The Fox and Hounds!'*

In the 1930s the Prince of Wales, later to become Edward VIII for ten months before he abdicated and lived abroad as the Duke of Windsor, visited Brook House which was then owned by the Measures family who kept a large racing stable. He attended the Point to Point Races which were held at that time.

*The Prince of Wales at the Point to Point*

Eric Williams, well known author of wartime novels lived for a year at the Porters Lodge, at the bottom of the drive to Melchbourne House, while writing one of his books. During the Second World War he had been shot down over Germany and imprisoned in Stalag Luft III on the German-Polish border. He escaped and returned to England, where he was awarded the Military Cross. His book, "The Wooden Horse", sold over a million copies and was made into a film.

Mary Frampton wrote "Forty Years On" in 1919 all about Riseley, although she disguised it and changed the names of the inhabitants.

Julia Jarman, author of over 70 books for children, lives on the High Street. Three of her adventure stories are set in Riseley and people will recognise names, pets, places and sometimes people. In "When Poppy Ran Away", Abe, the woodcutter is an affectionate portrait of Nev Cowley, who looked after Flints Wood for many years. The old vicarage is on the cover of "Poppy and the Vicarage Ghost". Laurie Gell, hero of "The Ghost of Tantony Pig" which looks back to a time when there was a pig farm where 131B High Street now stands and a blacksmith's forge on the other side of the road, has the name of a local family.

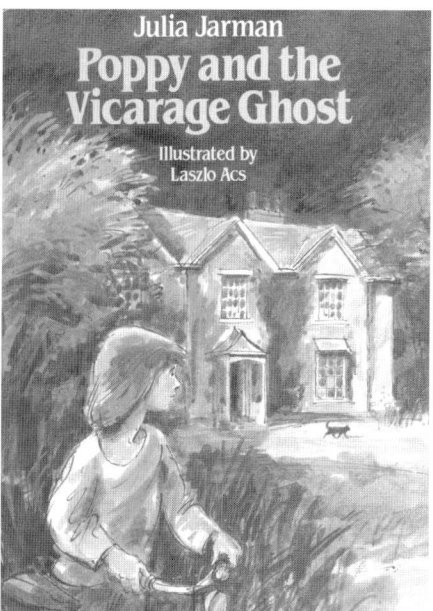 

*Book covers featuring Riseley people and places*

Sir David Putnam the film director came to the village to film the opening scene of "Defence of the Realm", starring Denholm Elliot. The scene involved a night time car chase, which started outside the Margaret Beaufort School and went towards Swineshead. The mobile film units, vehicles, caravans and actors were based in front of the school and filming went on throughout the night.

# Sport, Parades and Village Events
Andrew Gell and Peter Smith

### Football
Historians believe that about 2000 years ago the Chinese played a game that involved kicking a ball. In ancient Rome a kind of football was encouraged as a part of military training and subsequently was probably introduced into Britain during their occupation of these islands. The first historical account of an actual game being played was in London on Shrove Tuesday 1175. Subsequently these Shrove Tuesday games became notorious as *'mob football'* in which hundreds of youths chased a ball through streets with little regard for people or property. This led to the banning of the game by Edward III in 1314. Another reason for this restriction on football and other games too, was that it interfered with archery practice by the boys and men of towns and villages. Football survived, however, but was frowned upon by the church as can be seen in an abstract from the Archdeacon's Court book of 1611, when a William Sharpe of the village of Riseley was referred for, *'being about football on Ascension Day'*.

However, in 1617 James I declared the playing of games lawful, provided they were played after church service. Actual football clubs began to be formed in the 1820s. Several kinds of the game developed particularly in English independent schools and when students went to University they needed a unified set of rules. A standard code was drawn up at Cambridge in 1846 and revised in 1862 with ten rules. A year later, English clubs got together to form the Football Association, the rest as they say is history.

Amateur clubs sprang up all over the country and in 1885 the first professional clubs appeared and formed the foundation of the game as we know it today.

In Riseley, amateur football, as we have seen was played from the 17th century and like other villages, teams were formed and played in local leagues. During World War Two there were friendly games with other villages and as Eric Rootham remembers, *'we had Italian POWs in the village during the war and matches were often with them. It was rumoured*

*Riseley Football Club, 1920-21*
*Back row: Reverend Dodds, Stanley Litchfield, George Gell, Joseph Dickens, Ernest Porter*
*Middle row: Horace Rootham, Walter Hancock, Aubrey Savage*
*Seated: Charles Gell, Dick Carrington, 'Clary' Bateman, Abanarida (from Siam), Richard Sawford*

*1986-87 Division 5 Champions*
*Back row: Matthew Jackson, Gary Mitchell, Peter Thomas, Ryan Surridge, Stephen Prowse, Brian Gallagher, Derek Curtis*
*Front row: Richard Giles, Keith Ridley, Richard Ridley, Nigel Gell, Robin Randall, David Thompson*

*that they had two or three players who had played internationally for Italy before the war.'*

Riseley football continues to flourish with Saturday and Sunday teams competing in local leagues.

Matthew Jackson lived with his parents at 38 High Street. His father Andy, and Robin Gardner, started Saturday morning football coaching for under 10s in the 1970s. Matthew became an outstanding player who played for England Under 16s, Under 18s and Under 21s. He became a professional footballer and received a Cup Final Winners Medal in 1995 when Everton won the Cup. He is now captain of Norwich City.

**Cricket**
The origins of the game are obscure, but it was probably played in some form as early as the 1300s. It is thought that shepherd boys were the early exponents of the game using their crooks or cricks to hit a ball bowled at the wicker gate of a sheep-pen. This subsequently became known as the wicket. In its earliest form the ball was bowled underarm and bats were shaped liked hockey sticks. In the mid-1800s over arm bowling became legal and batsmen began using bats like those of today. The game was undoubtedly played in Riseley at an early date, but unfortunately records do not survive for that time and the first mention of the game in Riseley is in newspaper articles.

Within living memory, the first pitch was in Bowers Lane and as 'Steve' Stevens, Les Hawkins and Gilbert Barker all remember, *'we used to go there on Friday evenings to clear the cow-pats off the pitch ready for the Saturday game'*. As Jack Hancock recalls, *'if you didn't help to clear it up – you did not get to play'*.

One Riseley villager deserves a mention here. Thomas Carter *'Dickie'* Dodds was the son of the vicar in the 1920s and grew up in the old vicarage, which had a tennis court and cricket nets. The vicar had a love of the game and could bowl with both his left and right arm. The gardener at the vicarage at that time was Wilfred Gell who happened also to be the village fast bowler. He would leave his duties in the garden (with Revd Dodds' approval) and bowl at Dickie in the nets.

Dickie eventually went on to play for Warwickshire and then subsequently for Essex, where he played 380 matches from 1946-1959. By the end of his career he had on 13 occasions scored 1000 runs in a season.

*Riseley Cricket team, circa 1950*
*Back Row: Jack Hutchins, John Baines, Cecil Holmes, Bill Pell?, Len Stringer, Len Wildman, Alan Ellis*
*Sitting: Wyndham Partridge, Gerald Woolston, Jack Ashpole, George Hopkins, Bill Norman, Bill Allan*

**Point to Point**
A group of hunting men reined up their horses by a village church with a steeple. One of them rose in his saddle and pointed with his riding crop to another church steeple in the distance. *'I'll race you to that point,'* he said. Putting their horses into a gallop, the men streamed across the countryside to the mark. They called their sport a point to point race or steeple-chasing, and it soon became so popular that it became an annual event. Crowds gathered to watch and wager on the result. The chase across fields, over hedges, ditches and gates was turned into an organised race. The name of steeple-chasing and point to point racing stuck and remains to this day.

During the 1920s and 1930s the biggest event in the sporting calendar for Riseley was undoubtedly the point to point races organised by the Oakley Hunt. Held in early spring on a Thursday, which was the day that shops closed for the afternoon, it has been estimated to have attracted between 20,000 and 30,000 people each year. Many villagers alive today remember the High Street as being one long procession of cars. This may not seem surprising today, but in those times most people did not own a car and it must have been quite a sight.

*Procession of cars leaving the Point to Point*

The whole population usually turned out and the school in Church Lane was closed for the day. The course was over three miles and included 20 or so obstacles which were made up of brush fences, open and water jumps. There were usually five races including a ladies race. Professional riders were not allowed to compete. Admission to the course was free but the charge for car parking varied from £1 in the early days to £2 by the late 30s. Local people charged 6d (2$^1$/$_2$p) for parking bicycles in their front gardens – it was cheaper than taking them to the course. There were refreshment and beer tents as well as some small attractions such as jugglers and pedlars. Jack Hancock and others remember one particular sideshow; *'there was this one-legged man who attracted quite a bit of attention by performing the high jump. It was amazing the height this chap could clear.'*

Riseley – Our Village

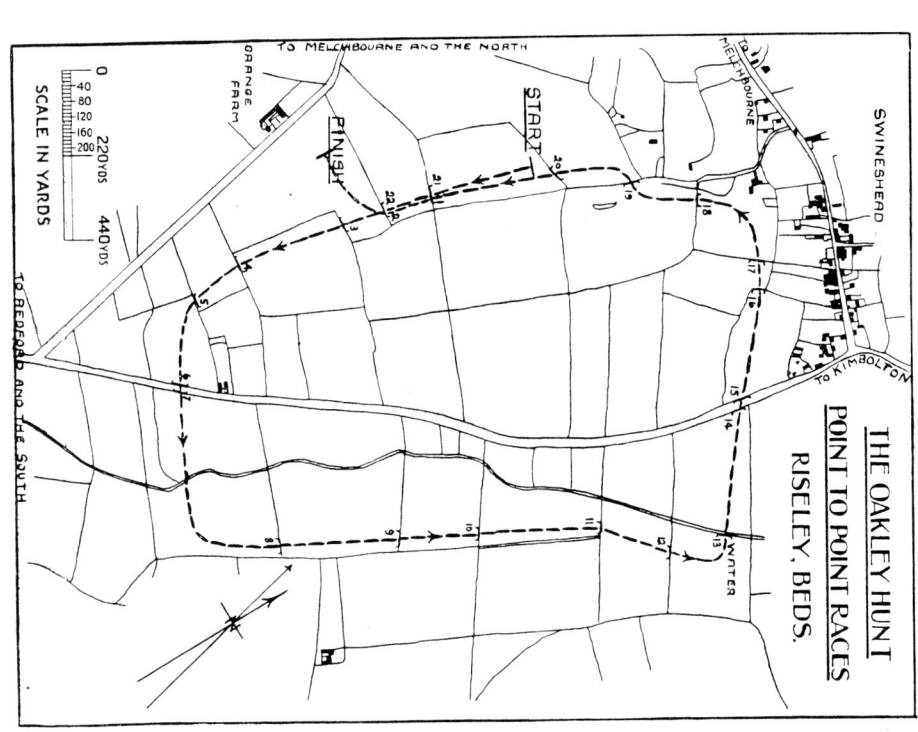

A Programme for the Point to Point, showing the course

## Sport, Parades and Village Events

*The start and finish of the Point to Point, opposite Grange Farm*

Harry Walker and other boys at the time would earn a few coppers collecting and returning beer glasses. One particular part of the course was reserved for the bookmakers, and their stands made a colourful sight with their different umbrellas. In one particular year in the early 1930s, the Prince of Wales, the future King Edward V111, came and participated in one of the races. As 'Steve' Stevens remembers, 'he

*A juggler performing at the Point to Point*

199

*attracted quite a lot of attention, of course, but unfortunately he came off his horse while attempting to clear the brook!'* In 1935 a light aeroplane landed nearby on the day of the race and it has always been rumoured within the village that its pilot was none other than Amy Johnson the famous aviator.

The Riseley point to point races were a massive event for the village and they continued until the outbreak of war in 1939.

**Bowls**

*The bowling green at The White Horse, with 'Clary' Bateman, Jack and Becket Hancock*

Flat green bowls dates back to ancient Egypt, Greece and Rome. It has flourished in England since the 1100s. Riseley bowling green was laid after the First World War and was situated in the field adjacent to the Old White Horse. It had three rinks and a small pavilion and the thriving membership paid a nominal rent of one shilling (5p) a year to a local brewery who owned the land.

## Sport, Parades and Village Events

*'Clary' Bateman, George Stoves and Arthur Batchelor at the bowling green*

At the conclusion of matches the members would go to The White Horse for refreshment. Occasionally dinners and prize-giving ceremonies were also held there. The trophies competed for were the Challenge Cup and the Partridge Cup.

There was a ladies section too with competitions running from 1934 to the 1950s. In the late 1960s the brewery was considering selling the land for development and consequently the green had to go. It was a sad loss to the village, but when the new village hall opened in 1979, a new generation of bowlers started to play indoor bowls. Originally there were about a dozen players each week. The numbers grew and now the club meets on Thursday evenings. Matches are played against other clubs.

The old Challenge Cup was presented to Riseley Indoor Bowls Club and is now known as the Captain's Cup. It is awarded annually to the member who, in the opinion of the captain, has made a great contribution to the club in the past year.

*Annual presentation evening for the Indoor Bowls Club*

## Badminton

Before the opening of the new village hall, in 1979, only a few enthusiastic villagers played badminton – either in Bedford or Rushden. The building of the hall was seen by them as an opportunity to bring the game to Riseley. The idea quickly gained support and so the hall was designed to incorporate the minimum height requirement for matches and a Granwood floor, laid for safety and for its hardwearing qualities.

The first club to form was the Tuesday Club. This was for experienced players, keen to play matches. They joined the Rushden League in the bottom division, as the rules decreed, and played their way steadily to the top. Their success has subsequently ebbed and flowed, but their enthusiasm has remained unshaken. Young players were brought on by Ian Smith's junior coaching. Not only did this ensure a squad of young players to augment the team, it also produced several excellent county players.

The Wednesday Club and the Monday Ladies' Club played some matches, but emphasised the enjoyable rather than the competitive side of the game. Some ladies played during the day as well as in the evening. Riseley still provides a base for the Wanderers – a peripatetic ladies' team. Many villagers of all ages have joined in this sport and enjoyed the opportunity provided by the facilities for badminton in the village hall.

**The Intervillage Sports Competition** – Barbara Jones
During the 1980s, Riseley could justly boast that it was Bedfordshire's premiere sporting small village. From 1983 to 1987 the Sports Council, Eastern Region, held an intervillage sports competition and Riseley became county champions every year. The village entered the small village section – under 1000 residents – and had to compete in five a-side football, netball, badminton (mixed doubles) and table tennis (singles and mixed doubles) at junior and senior level, and darts at senior level only. To finish off, there was an obstacle relay demanding speed, balance and a variety of skills. It was this relay that dramatically decided Riseley as county winner in the very first competition. It also established an annual event in the Riseley calendar and a fierce rivalry with the village of Stevington.

Becoming Bedfordshire's champions meant a weekend at the Eurosports Centre at Shotley, near Ipswich, to challenge the village champions from all the other eastern region counties. There were 42 in the team and the few remaining seats in the coach were keenly contested by an army of supporters. Financial support came from village donations, sponsorship and the Parish Council. It provided the expenses and the unique *'designer label'* Riseley T-shirts.

The weekend was a great success. The event brought together a cross section of the village and the sportsmanship, determination to win and team spirit epitomised all that sport should be about. The sun shone and the Saturday night disco revealed incredible funds of energy from those who a few hours earlier seemed to have given their all.

Late on Sunday afternoon the team was jubilant when they came third – in a very close finish. The trophies for that and subsequent competitions are on display at The Fox and Hounds.

The following year's competition had a lot to live up to. Riseley beat Stevington to regain the county title! Hopes were high as the team set off for Shotley, but from arrival it was obvious that the organisation of the event was poor and when the food ran out at dinner on Saturday night it left several late finishing teams hungry and so disgruntled that not even the disco could lift their spirits. The next day brought an all-time early breakfast as everyone was determined to make sure of their meal. It began a day of closely fought matches and again, the relay to decide a close final position. This time Riseley was 4th.

*Some of the team and supporters waiting for the results: Shotley 1983*
*Back row: Stephanie Hodgson, Maureen Allen, Wendy Lightfoot, Brian Lightfoot, James Lightfoot, Vic Scrivener, Chris Haseman*
*Front row: Mary Dring, Jackie Gardner, Mary Haseman, Barbara Jones, Pauline Scrivener, Jane Rhodes, Jack Childs*

There were changes in 1985. Alec Cohen took over as team manager from Barbara Jones and the Sports Council changed the venue to a sports centre in Ipswich. This meant that there was no built-in accommodation and the team had to stay in a hotel. It naturally increased the cost and having become Bedfordshire's champions again (beating Stevington) it was only after a successful search for sponsorship that the village was able to continue. Other villages felt this too and it was the last year that the event took place over two days. In 1986 and 1987 it was a one day event. 1987 also saw the introduction of rounders, making a very full schedule.

There was still great enjoyment of the events and a wonderful spirit of competition, although because so many matches had to be played simultaneously it was difficult for the teams to support one another. A loyal band of supporters still followed the team, yet the sideline atmosphere was inevitably changing.

But Riseley was on the up. In 1985 they were 5th, in 1986 4th and in 1987 a very heroic 3rd.

And there the competition ended. The Sports Council lost its overall sponsor and the tournament finished. Who knows, in another two years Riseley might have climbed to the top. But what mattered was that for five years the Sports Council achieved its aims – enjoyable sport for all, founded on true community spirit.

**Walter Howard**
Walter Howard, brother of Jack Howard of Daintry Farm was famous as a runner in the 1920s and 1930s. Having taken part in village sporting events as a boy, he joined the Kettering Harriers. He took part in competitions all over the country and won the All England Championship for Cross Country Running.

**Feast Sunday**

*Riseley Feast Parade returning from the church at Gold Street bridge, circa 1930*

Riseley – Our Village

Feast Sunday was the Sunday following the 19 July. Scouts came from surrounding villages and many from Rushden. They paraded up the High Street to the church for a special service. Then a further parade back to the High Street from where they disbanded to the homes of villagers for a slap up tea.

Children took produce and gifts to the church which were then taken to Bedford Hospital.

**The Moravian Annual Party**
The Moravian annual party followed the special anniversary service of the Moravian Chapel. The party was held in the field where Paulsons Close is now. A treat for the children would be the throwing of sweets into the air by the chapel elders. All the children from the village would scrabble for them. Today, the pleasure gained from this may seem difficult to imagine but in those days families were poor and the chance of free sweets caused great excitement.

*The Moravian Party, circa 1920. 105 High Street and its barns in the background*

**The Annual Children's Party**
A children's party was held in the old village hall every January. It was a great event – cakes, jellies and all the favourite party games.

Often an entertainer was hired and the instruction to attendees was *'bring your own spoon and mug'*!

*Annual Children's Party circa 1960*

## Coronation of King George V, 1911

*Villagers in fancy dress with decorated bicycles celebrate the coronation*

*Procession at Gold Street bridge to celebrate the coronation*

## Coronation of Queen Elizabeth II, June 1953

It was a very wet day for the Coronation parade. Where villagers had decorated their houses with red, white and blue crepe paper bunting the colour ran so that for weeks afterwards the houses were stained in patriotic colours.

*A ship float just passing 93 High Street*

Sport, Parades and Village Events

*A tractor towed float outside 78 High Street – the old steps and shutters are no longer there*

Following the parade there was a display of fireworks and a torchlight procession up to the site of the old windmill at the top of Mill Hill where a huge bonfire was lit.

**The Friendly Societies**
Another important feature of village life in the late 19th century and the early part of the 20th were two Friendly Societies. The Ancient Order of Foresters and the Independent Order of Odd Fellows.

These friendly societies are still in existence today and in simple terms were insurance based organisations whose function was to provide income in the event of sickness or accident and to provide money towards the cost of medical and dental treatment. There was no welfare state in those days. They also provided life insurance and mortgage facilities.

These organisations were divided into lodges and the members used the term *'brothers'*. They met once a quarter with the Ancient Order of Foresters meeting in The Royal Oak and the Odd Fellows meeting at The Five Bells. They were open to men only. The members paid their subscriptions at the quarterly meetings. Initial payment for initiation into the friendly societies was relatively expensive for the times. To join the Odd Fellows for example cost 5s 3d (26½p) in 1842 rising to between 12s (60p) and 18s (90p) in 1879 depending on age at entry.

*The Foresters posing for a photograph in full regalia outside The Royal Oak*

*The parade forming up at the junction of Keysoe Road. Note the regalia of the leading village members, circa 1910-1912*

Sport, Parades and Village Events

Most of the men in the village would have been members of one or other society. A local person would act as the lodge secretary to do the book keeping for subscriptions and claims to be paid.

*The parade in later years processing past The Fox and Hounds*

*The parade in Gold Street*

Each year the friendly societies paraded to the church for a special service. The banner in the photographs above is for the Ancient Order of Foresters.

211

## The Annual Fair

This was a great annual event, which was held on the village green – the area in front of The Five Bells and the grass areas opposite. It was at its heyday in the years leading up to World War One and it is during that period in which the following photographs were taken.

*Children at the annual fair*

*Soldiers in uniform enjoying the fair, circa 1914*

The steam powered *'gallopers'* were Christopher Smiths' steam galloping horses. In addition to the ride there were stalls and sideshows and treats such as Domenicos pure ice cream. Sadly, this annual event ceased after the First World War

*Merry-go-round outside The Five Bells*

*Maypole dancing in the field adjacent to Riseley Lodge Farm, Bowers Lane, around 1935*

*'Hooking the bottles', circa 1935*

*Harry Brown climbing the greasy pole around 1925*

Visiting fairs and circuses came to the village into the 1960s but not on the scale of the earlier fairs on the green.

**The Floods**
A regular natural event in the life of the village is the flooding of the brook. Periods of heavy rain, winter or summer, cause the brook to

## Sport, Parades and Village Events

overflow into the High Street, bringing pleasure to the children but misery to those who have the water in their houses. It was and is possible to negotiate the flood at The Fox and Hounds by heading for the pavement side of the street where the water is not so deep.

*Russ Warren, the butcher, negotiating the flood*

*Floods in 1992*

*An early picture of flooding at Gold Street bridge*

*Jock Wesley riding his horse through a flood in about 1960. This photograph shows Mrs Seebon leaning against the fence outside her shop and in the background the brick outbuildings of one of the village bakeries – Tom Valentine's*

# Our Village
**Florence Wilkinson**

### The Village Hall
Before Riseley had its own village hall, there were various Reading Rooms, which were used for meetings and communal activities. One of them was a building, now replaced by The Barns. Another was at what is now 78 High Street. There were steps up to the entrance from the street and instead of the windows that are there now, there were ancient shuttered windows and a door (see the building in the illustration on page 209). There was another known as the British Legion Room behind 40 High Street, formerly The Boot.

The first village hall in Riseley was built after the First World War. When the men came back from serving in the army, they donated their gratuity to pay for the hall. It was built on land opposite the Post Office where 98A and 98B High Street now stand. The land was donated by Lord St John.

*Old Village Hall – between Cobblestones and Dorville House*

It was built on piers and grew from a fairly small wooden hut to a larger one. It was a cold place in the winter, despite the coke stoves which were installed. In 1951 Messrs T A Saul Ltd bought Lord St John's property in Riseley, as well as several farms in the surrounding area and the hall, as it was then, was formally given to the village.

The hall was looked after by a committee voted for by the village. Toilets were installed when mains drainage came through the village in 1955-56. The hall became the meeting place for many organisations as well as the venue for private parties and wedding receptions. Eventually it was realised that the hall was coming to the end of its life and the committee set about raising money to build a new one.

Many were the events held to raise cash. Avenues were explored too, in which organisations such as the County Council were able to help. The County Council finally gave the village £1 for every £1 raised, and at last the sum of £55,000, together with grant aid was raised. The new village hall was built in Gold Street, on the site of the tennis court which was seldom used by the villagers and was in a very poor state. The ground belonged to the village, being part of the playing field.

*To Commemorate the opening of*
RISELEY VILLAGE HALL
*on Saturday, 8th September, 1979 by Councillor Mrs. Anthony Polhill*

*Programme for Opening of Village Hall*

The hall was commissioned and was opened on 8 September, 1979 by Mrs Anthony Polhill in the presence of a large crowd of villagers including the committee who had worked so hard.

In the following years committees have spent time and money, as well as considerable effort in improving the facilities available to the village.

*The New Village Hall*

**The Playing Field**

The need for a playing field had been discussed during the war but the first step was not taken until June 1946, when the Parish Council decided to buy the field known as Parkinson's Close. At a Parish meeting in September of that year the Playing Field Committee was formed to raise the money needed so that the project would not be a financial liability to the ratepayers.

Negotiations with the Ministry of Education, through the Bedfordshire Playing Fields Association, for assistance under the Physical Recreation and Training Act 1937, secured the promise of a grant of 60% of the original estimated expenditure.

Work started early in 1949 and by March 1950 the village had the use of a hard tennis court and five acres of grass, including a turfed cricket table and a full size Association Football pitch. The car park was ready by spring 1951.

A set of four swings, the first part of the children's corner was erected in April 1952. The Bedfordshire Education Committee provided half the cost of this, and as the school children used the field for physical education they undertook to keep the grass cut.

The final cost of the whole project including purchase, levelling, drainage and provision of present facilities amounted to £2,800. An increased grant of £1,450 from the Ministry of Education, together with £100 from the Education Committee and £25 from the Playing Fields Association left the village to raise £1,225 themselves. The Playing Fields Association also gave an interest free loan of £150.

The activities of the Cricket, Football and Tennis Clubs and the use of the field were sufficient satisfaction for the many who had worked during the past six years.

The field was officially opened by the Rt Hon Lord Luke of Pavenham, on Saturday 20 September, 1952.

In 1964 a formal agreement was made between the Parish Council and the Riseley Recreational Association, for the day to day running of the playing field. These organisations have worked together over the years to ensure that the field is maintained in good order. The Borough Council has given grants for new equipment and for safety surfacing to be installed in a continuing programme of improvements.

*Souvenir programme for the opening of Riseley Playing Field*

**The Newsletter** – Deborah Abel, Editor 1993-2000
The Village Newsletter is produced once every two months and aims to report on recent happenings within the village, to inform residents on wider county issues, to gather support for forthcoming events and to chat about village life in general. It would not be possible without the support of Riseley Parish Council, who pay all the printing and distribution costs to ensure that it is received by every householder in the village.

The Newsletter has existed in its current form since the spring of 1993, only in those days it was one folded sheet (now it can be as many as five!) and I stumbled into the role of editor quite by chance. Having lived at *'The Ramblers'* in the High Street for over 15 years, I remember enjoying a typed village news sheet produced by Roger Phillips and being disappointed when it stopped arriving. After tackling two Parish Councillors on the subject, I was told that it had stopped because they could not find a replacement editor and since I obviously felt so passionately about the important role the Newsletter had to play in the village . . . that I was perfect for the job! Despite my protestations that I had no time to spare and no computer or typewriter on which to produce the first copy, I was told that I had beautiful handwriting and that, *'the busy person always finds time to fit in one more thing!'* and so it began!

Over the years interest in the Newsletter has grown – as always there is minimal editorial input, material is provided by village groups and organisations. Despite the dawn of a new millennium, the Newsletter continues to be written by hand due to popular public demand! Perhaps the bold print makes it easy for people of all ages to read and gives it that all important personal touch. I see the Newsletter as an important link drawing together our rather spread out village into a community and lots of positive feedback suggests that it is widely appreciated. I hope the Newsletter will long continue with its current support and success and that there will always be some sort of village communication into the distant future.

**Policing in Riseley**
Policing in rural Bedfordshire was formalised in the Victorian era. The old grouping of petty session by hundreds, which began in the days

before the Domesday Book, was dispensed with in 1830. The three northern hundreds – the Stodden Hundred which included Riseley, the Willey Hundreds which included Thurleigh, Sharnbrook and surrounding parishes and the Buckley Hundred which included Bletsoe, Ravensden, Bromham, Stevington, Biddenham and Stagsden were combined into one petty sessional district. The centre was to be at Bletsoe, but was actually located at Sharnbrook where a courthouse and cells were built. Riseley was then policed from Sharnbrook.

Riseley had a resident policeman in the early 1900s. Sergeant Crowsley, father of Charlie Crowsley, lived at 76 High Street. The house had a police notice board, but otherwise was a private house with no office or provision for carrying out police business.

*Sergeant Crowsley outside Cherry Trees, 76 High Street*

A police house was built in Riseley in 1928 – 131 High Street. This did have an office and villagers could call to report crime and discuss other matters of concern to the police. There were no cells, and it was the family home of the local constable. In the 1970s, when the practice of providing housing for police officers was phased out, 131 High Street was sold into private ownership. Policing was then carried out from Bedford and Kempston with panda cars replacing the bobby on his cycle.

Our Village

*The police house – 131 High Street*

In the late 1990s it became a requirement to have a police presence in the villages of North Bedfordshire. The Instrument Engineering workshop, which was vacant, offered suitable accommodation and so it was purchased and fitted out. The police post was officially opened in April 1999. Although it is not manned 24 hours per day, it is a base which allows officers to respond more quickly to incidents in the North Bedfordshire villages.

*The new police post*

223

**Parish Council** – Andrew Gell

As mentioned in the chapter on All Saints Church, the church vestry meetings used to have powers relating to the running of the village. This all changed in 1894 with the passing, by Parliament, of the Local Government Act. This act required parishes to elect a Parish Council to administer village affairs and transferred the duties, other than those relating to the church, to the Parish Council. The Act required this change to be effective from 31 December 1894.

Accordingly a meeting of parochial electors was held in the schoolroom at 7.00 pm on 4 December 1894. Ninety-two electors were present. Revd Turner was elected chairman for the meeting. He was proposed by Joseph Gell, seconded by Charles Savage and received 36 votes. The schoolmaster at the time, Mr Hewitt was proposed by David Waldock and seconded by Tom Valentine, but only received 32 votes.

Nomination Papers were called for, from those wishing to become one of the nine new Parish Councillors. Thirty nominations were received, but six then withdrew. A show of hands for each nomination produced the following result:

| Thomas Adams | 30 | John Lowe | 1 |
| --- | --- | --- | --- |
| Joseph Bailey | 0 | Bani Rootham | 14 |
| Charles Belton | 7 | Daniel Rootham | 45 |
| Thomas Birch | 20 | Charles Savage | 22 |
| Duncan Bower | 53 | Karrington Shore | 12 |
| George Childs | 40 | Stephen Stevens | 42 |
| Isaac Dickens | 35 | Maximilian Townley | 15 |
| Samuel Ekins | 62 | Tom Valentine | 34 |
| Joseph Gell | 14 | Joseph Wagstaff | 27 |
| Charles Johnson | 19 | S Westley | 22 |
| Eli Litchfield | 29 | William Wildman | 23 |
| John W Lowe | 10 | William Wyant | 17 |

However, instead of the top nine being elected to the first Parish Council, a poll was demanded by the electors present and a date of 17 December was agreed. Twenty-two of the original 24 put their names forward and the results were announced by the returning officer on 18

December as Messrs Ekins, Bower, Rootham, Adams, Childs, Litchfield, Stevens, Townley and Johnson. The very first Parish Council meeting was held on 31 December 1894.

Parish Council meetings are still held in the schoolroom and there are still nine Parish Councillors who come up for re-election every four years. As in 1894, Parish Councillors give their time free in carrying out these duties. The main function of the Parish Council is to represent the village on any matter relating to the parish, in dealing with the Bedford Borough Council, Bedfordshire County Council and Government Agencies. It is directly responsible for street lighting and the grass cutting within the village and is owner, on behalf of the village, of the playing field and Ross Meadow.

The money required for administering the village is calculated by the Parish Council annually in November or December and is called the precept. The amount is then advised to the Borough Council and is included in the Council Tax for Riseley residents.

In the year 2000, the Parish Councillors are: David Balderstone, Ruth Clark, Sheila Copping, Andrew Gell, Iain Harding, Ann Hughes, Michael Ives, Jon Powell and Mary Shiers. The Parish Clerk is Kate Latham, our Borough Councillor is Ian Clifton and our County Councillor is A P Hendry.

**Margaret Beaufort Middle School**
On Monday 13 July 1964 Margaret Beaufort Middle School was officially declared open by the Honourable Pearl Lawson-Johnston. County Alderman W G Matthews, who owned the village shop at one time, was Chairman of the Governing body and made the reply at the opening ceremony.

The Director of Education wrote: *'Margaret Beaufort School was built as part of the Authority's rural reorganisation programme, under which the all-age schools were to be discontinued. The opening of the school in September 1962, enabled the Local Education authority to reorganise the all-age Primary Schools at Keysoe, Riseley and Sharnbrook as Junior and Infant Schools. Secondary education for children of 11 years of age and over who reside in the villages of Bletsoe, Bolnhurst, Dean, Felmersham, Keysoe, Knotting, Little*

Staughton, Melchbourne, Pertenhall, Riseley, Sharnbrook, Shelton, Souldrop, Swineshead, Thurleigh and Yelden is now provided for by Margaret Beaufort School in conjunction with Pilgrim School and the Harpur Trust Schools in Bedford and by Kimbolton School.'*

The County Architect at the time explained the rationale behind the design and building of the school:

*'Because the Royal Aircraft Establishment wind tunnels and testing beds are sited on the plateau above Riseley Village, a site was chosen low enough to afford some protection by the escarpment against noise. The School site is in fact some 70 feet below the testing area. Further special precautions needed to be taken against penetration of excessive noise, and absorbing any of the noise which did so penetrate. Thus the buildings are built of unusually heavy construction, the openings in external walls have been kept as small as possible, windows are doubleglazed. Rooms have ceilings and floors of high sound absorbent materials. Mechanical ventilation is provided so that, on days of testing, the windows may remain closed and still provide the air change required by the School Building Regulations.*

*The plan . . . is unusual in its compactness – being a simple rectangle of concrete with the rooms filling the whole of the area. This type of plan has made for a minimum of circulation space and resulted in economies, freeing money to cover the cost of the special construction.*

*The Swimming pool is, in fact, the static water supply tank required by the County Fire Service for fire fighting needs, to which a chlorinating and filter plant has been added.*

*The School was built at a cost of £96,000 by Messrs Samuel Foster Ltd of Kempston.'*

The school is named after Lady Margaret Beaufort, who was born at Bletsoe Castle in 1441 and stayed there on many occasions with her step brother Lord St John. The emblem chosen for the school is hers – the marguerite flower.

The school was originally designed for 2 forms of entry. It had 8 classrooms, a library, science and rural science laboratories, rooms for domestic science, needlework, art and handicraft and a hall/gymnasium, all equipped for the teaching of courses up to the old GCE level.

*Margaret Beaufort School*

The school has gone through a number of changes, especially in 1977, when as part of a countywide reorganisation, it became a middle school for pupils aged 9 – 13. The following two decades have seen further changes including the updating and conversion of rooms to comply with the needs of the National Curriculum, which was introduced in 1988 and the provision of three mobile classrooms.

Margaret Beaufort has proved a popular school. The number on roll has increased from 200 to 360. On leaving the school at 13, pupils transfer to Sharnbrook Upper School. This unusual form of three tier educational provision is increasingly rare in England, but continues to flourish in North Bedfordshire.

## Scouting and Guiding

The 24th (Riseley) Scout Group was first registered in July 1911 – one of the County's earliest. It continued with unbroken service until 1939. It was one of the originals when the group system came into being in 1927-28 and was also one of the very few groups in North Bedfordshire to register a Rover Scout Crew 1927-28.

*Riseley Scout Band outside Daintry House*

The Scout Troop was present at Princess Mary's Rally, Russell Park, Bedford, 14 July 1928, and the Jamborally, Ampthill Park, Whitsun 1933, when a visit was made by the Chief Scout and Chief Guide Lord and Lady Baden Powell.

Often, Riseley would be the site for weekend camps by groups from Bedford and the scouts would attend church parades in Riseley and other surrounding villages. The group was disbanded due to the lack of scouters just before the outbreak of the Second World War and not re-registered until 1967.

In 1967 the then vicar of Riseley, the Revd Fred Davis, considered that it was time that scouting was restarted in the village. A public meeting was called in the village hall, with Major Simon Whitbread in the chair.

It was found that there was a big enough response by both boys and parents, to make a viable group in the village, with support from the surrounding villages. The then District Commissioner, the Revd Henderson-Begg, went away to check on a number of volunteers. Mr John Grover was appointed Group Scout Leader and the parent committee was formed. Things progressed from there with the formation of the cub pack and the scout troop. The group has had varied fortunes over the years with the troop fluctuating from about 15 boys down to zero when the troop was closed for a while. The cub pack has always run well with a succession of leaders and with varying degrees of success in many fields. Within the sports field the pack was very successful in the tug-o-war where for many years they were unbeatable; they also had varied results in the remainder of the sports days.

In 1979 the group sent Martyn Shaw and Steve Jackson to the World Jamboree in Canada where they made many contacts in the scouting world. When they came back they passed on their experiences to the rest of the group.

All sections of Riseley Scout Group are currently well represented in many District and County events, always giving of their best and making a name for themselves.

In recent years the group has been thriving. A Beaver Section has a membership of 18, Cubs 21 and the Scouts 33. The scout troop now includes 11 girls following changes implemented in line with Scout Association policy.

In summer 2000 the scout troop held its summer camp at the Kandersteg International Scout Centre in Switzerland. In addition to this, all three sections camped together for the Millennium District Camp at Carlton in May 2000.

**1st Riseley Guide Company and 1st Riseley Brownie Pack**
It is thought Mrs Maisie Curtis started the guide company in 1946 and the brownie pack followed later.

On the guide company's 21st Birthday, in 1967, a celebration party was held for the guides, brownies, commissioners, helpers, ex-guides and ex-brownies. Over 100 guests participated in the celebrations.

The guides and brownies have always attended the Remembrance Day Service at Riseley Church when the Union Flag and the Company Colour was carried. Mr Jack Hancock always laid the poppy wreath. Each year the guides and brownies gave the elderly people of the village a tea party and entertainment.

Some weeks before Christmas, Mrs Curtis would start rehearsals for the Christmas Nativity play held every year in the Lady Chapel at Riseley Church. As Mrs Curtis was leader of the guides, brownies and also took the Church Sunday School, she had a lot of children to fit in. It was always a beautiful and moving story of the Nativity.

In 1965, the guides were lucky enough to be in the Whitsun County Camp in Ampthill Park. The big thrill was that they were joined by the World Chief Guide, Lady Olave Baden-Powell who met and talked to many guides.

Mrs Curtis always gave the brownies and guides a great deal of help and support, as did her daughter Margaret who was a brownie and guide. The girls could always call at *'Captain's'* home in Gold Street. Whilst she was their leader, the Company gained three Queen's Guide awards – a great achievement.

After Mrs Curtis retired, the guides were taken over by Mrs Symmes of Yelden for a short time and then by Christine Futter in 1973 until 1987.

Among the many annual camps Mrs Futter took the guides to, was a long weekend camp at the East of England Showground at Peterborough in August 1983. There were guides from eleven East Anglian counties and many different Countries taking part and the girls were very lucky to have been able to attend. The blessing of the Anglia Standard took place on the Sunday afternoon. Brownies and guides who were not able to attend the camp came and visited for the day. The friendships, activities and atmosphere contributed to an experience they would never forget.

*Queen's Guides, 10 October 1983. Jennifer Chapman and Joanne Futter receive their awards from Joy Hall (centre), District Commissioner*

Mrs Barbara Middleton (nee Westley) then carried on the brownies as Brown Owl after being pack leader and Tawny Owl under Mrs Curtis. Mrs George from Melchbourne took over from Mrs Middleton.

The brownies are now led by Mrs Lynne Roddis and, there is always a full pack with a waiting list.

**Playgroups**
During the 1960s new homes, many designed for young couples and growing families, were built in Riseley. College estate began with five houses in College Drive and nine in Brooklands Road. Maple Gardens and Kings Close increased the number of houses. Some long-time villagers were unhappy about the influx of newcomers, but others welcomed them as a positive sign of a thriving village.

At the same time the National Playgroup Association was getting its message across about the needs of pre-school children and the value of play. Hilary Southcombe, a qualified nursery nurse with experience of playgroups was one of the first *'new mothers'* to move into the village.

With the support of a group of like-minded mothers, she set about opening a playgroup.

It took many coffee mornings, jumble sales and the ubiquitous Tupperware parties to raise the money to buy toys and get underway. In 1967 the playgroup opened in the Methodist hall in Wells Road. Children could enrol from the age of three (but not if they were still wearing nappies!) and left to start school (usually rising five). Mothers were expected to take their turn in supporting the paid, qualified staff.

The hall was always a bustle of activity. In fine weather bikes, tractors and milk floats raced around outside, while inside there was painting, craft activities, singing, percussion and dancing, as well as the quieter story time activities. Colder weather did bring its problems – defrosting the little milk bottles and inventing more warm-up exercises.

*The playgroup Nativity play, Christmas 1992. Standing: Tom Henman, Robert Eeuwens, Tiffany Ridley, Stephanie Bloodworth, Paula-Jane Zurewel Sitting: Alistair Povey, Eleanor Soden, Liam Dazley, Joanne McFiggins*

There were spin off activities from the twice weekly sessions. Swimming trips were organised and sometimes the children were taken to Margaret Beaufort School – then a secondary modern school – for the students to take care of them as part of their child care course.

There were Christmas parties with magicians and the annual nativity play which brought a tear to many an eye.

By the 1980s the group was flourishing with up to 30 children on roll and a healthy bank balance. The new village hall opened and the group transferred to this larger building. At the Lower School the nursery unit opened, extending state provision to four year olds. As the older children no longer attended, the playgroup widened its scope to include babies and toddlers. An afternoon session for mothers and their babies already took place, but now this was incorporated into the playgroup. The ethos of the group remained, but the activities were geared to younger children with plenty of free activity, craftwork and the very popular singing sessions. One day a week was retained for older unaccompanied children, to prepare them for nursery school, but the pendulum had swung and most sessions included mothers.

Times are changing and the increasing number of women taking maternity leave or returning to work has meant that the use of child minders and nursery units has increased. More women have cars and are no longer dependent on village facilities. The number of children in the Mother and Toddler Club is in decline, but the dedicated leaders are still active and many kitchens in the village still display Picasso-like pictures stuck to the fridge!

**Mothers' Union**
For many years the Mothers' Union was active in the village. It was run by the church and provided an opportunity for women in the village to get together. Outside speakers were invited to talk to the group, which met once a month. Mrs Paulson was the Presiding Member during the ministry of her husband, the Revd Paulson. However, he had to leave the parish owing to ill health and until the Revd Davis it was presided over by Mrs Perry, wife of the Revd Canon Perry of Bedford. However, Mrs Davis, wife of the new vicar, declined to take over the Presidency, so in 1957 the branch was suspended.

*The Mothers' Union – Left to right: Mrs Carrie Holmes, Mrs Filsell, Miss Shelford, Mrs Brooks, Mrs M Curtis, Mrs J Tomkins, Mrs Sheila Surridge, Mrs S Ball, Mrs N Ingle, Mrs Posnett with son Andrew*

## The WEA

There has been a branch of the Workers Education Association in Riseley ever since the end of the First World War when it was founded. This is run from Cambridge and although it is called the Sharnbrook branch, it has always met in Riseley. It meets once a week for $1^1/_2$ hours and the members choose the subjects for lecturers to speak on – canals and railways, literature, gardens and many other interesting subjects. This September the topic is "From Bodysnatchers to DNA"! They also hold an annual harvest supper and sale.

## The Women's Institute

The WI started in Stoney Creek, Ontario, Canada, in the late 19th century. It came to England and Wales in 1915. It started in Anglesey and spread across the rest of England. A branch started in Riseley in 1930. The members no longer make jam, which was one of the chief activities earlier, especially during the war years. There are now 45 members and it is a very lively and active organisation. There are regular meetings with a wide variety of interesting speakers. Outings are arranged to famous homes, such as Chatsworth House, to gardens,

Our Village

such as Kathy Brown's interesting garden in Stevington. Towards Christmas time there is usually a shopping trip. In the past there have been visits to factories, such as the Wedgewood factory at Barlaston, Staffordshire.

*The Women's Institute visit to the Wedgewood Factory – 1959.*
*Left to right, front row: Edith Savage, Florence Chapman, Kate Sharman, Elsie Litchfield, Evelyn Rootham, Florence Wilkinson*
*Second row: Betty Allen, Beatrice Porter, Florence Wise, Bella Stringer, May Felce*
*Third row: Gwen Savage, Mary Allan, Grace Taylor, Gwen Smith, Jennie Howard, Peggie Howard*
*Back row: Freda Childs, Doris Genn, Jane Genn*

Members have visited Denman College, a lovely Georgian hall near Oxford – the education centre for the WI. Others have attended conferences at various universities while the students are on vacation, and travelled to the European Parliament at Strasbourg and Brussels.

**Riseley Dramatic Society and the Riseley Players**
The Riseley Dramatic Society was founded after the Second World War and continued until the mid-1950s. Many people from the village took part, but Godfrey Measures was the driving force. He wrote some of the plays that were performed.

*Drama in the old village hall. Left to right – back row: June Tompkins, Jim Nicholls, Mrs Batchelor, Dorothy Nicholson, Godfrey Measures, Daphne Rootham, Jean Gilder, Dave Short
Front row: Jack Lea, Margaret Wildman, Phylis Batchelor, Norman Shakesby, Pearl Felce, Eric Rootham*

Every year a show was put on at the beginning of December, over Thursday, Friday and Saturday nights. The dress rehearsal was on the Wednesday night and a coach load of boys with disabilities came from Hinwick Hall to watch. This gave the boys a night out and was a valuable audience for the actors. The shows consisted of one act plays and sketches with a finale of songs from shows that were current – usually by Rodgers and Hammerstein or Ivor Novello. They were performed in the old village hall. It had a stage, but very little room to store props or for the actors to get changed. However, they managed and put on some fine performances. The hall did not have a piano, so a baby grand was hired for the week. Peggie Howard was the pianist. The shows were popular and the tickets sold very quickly.

Shows were also put on for one night in surrounding villages and occasionally in Rushden. Drama festivals were held in various towns and these were judged and cups awarded to the winners. Riseley Dramatic Society often took part in these festivals which were held in Bedford, Dunstable, Harpenden and St Albans. In 1948 Godfrey Measures' play "Spring Time for Mary" won the cup for the best original play. The group was disbanded in 1955.

The Riseley Players gave their first performance in 1981. The catalyst for the formation of the new group was Barry Agnew. The new village hall included new facilities and Barry, with the help of his wife Alison, decided to put on a village show. As Peter Allen recalls, *'he enlisted the musical talents of Tony Hague, the artistry of Chris Harrott and the technical skills of Pete Marston. He begged, bribed and bullied innocent and ertswhile retiring villagers into acting, singing and dancing. Like a fledgling bird, The Riseley Revue stirred, flexed its wings and finally took flight in April 1981. The show was full of delights. It included the Ladies Badminton Club showstoppers, somewhat bizarrely featuring Ian Smith. The first of many great Russell Woodward monologues and many great Phil Strickland comic performances appeared in this first programme. Carolyn Siddall directed "The Tram Track Tragedy", a genuine Victorian melodrama and Tony Jesson starred in the villainous role that was to type-cast him forever. The sight of so many of their fellow-villagers blissfully making complete fools of themselves captivated the audience.'*

Riseley – Our Village

A successful pantomime followed in December of the same year, but unfortunately, this was followed by a period of 18 months when no performances were mounted.

Fortunately, Enid Cooper arrived on the scene and was persuaded to take on the director's role. As Pete says, *'the great era of the Cooper directorate had dawned. For seven years The Riseley Players staged one success after another; plays, pantomimes, musical shows, revues. Two, sometimes three, productions a year, each one seemingly better than its predecessor. Enid herself took charge of most of them. Judy Ware, Russell Woodward, Brian Terry, Brian Green and, happily descended from the lofty heights of his Five Bells bar stool, the irreplaceable and hugely talented Colin James directed others. These were the happiest days.'*

In 1991, The Riseley Players produced Oliver – a great success and followed by – nothing. Until . . .

In 2000, just as this book was being put together, The Riseley Players put on their first show for nine years. It was a Variety Show under the hand of Enid Cooper. Audiences for the two nights were delighted to welcome her back, as well as so many of the original band of very talented actors and singers.

*Riseley Dramatic Society, summer 2000*
*Jean Morgan-Jones, Steph Griffiths, Isobel Kennedy, Doreen Graham, Marilyn Harries, Rene Presland, Debbie Swallow, Phil Strickland, Judy Ware*

Riseley has several other small organisations which enhance the lives of villagers. **Meals on Wheels** was started by the Women's Royal Voluntary Service (WRVS) in 1966. Elderly or infirm people are eligible and currently three meals a week are delivered. The meals have been supplied by public houses, the post office at Keysoe and even by private individuals. Now the food is cooked in the school kitchen at Margaret Beaufort School.

**The Over 60s Club** meets monthly at the village hall and has various speakers. Every year there is a Christmas dinner which all villagers over 60 years of age can attend. Father Christmas also comes, complete with a sack of gifts!

Recently the **Luncheon Club** has been formed. This is for elderly residents and meets in the day centre at Brook House once a fortnight. Attendance has been increasing steadily since the first meeting.

**The Wine Club** started in Riseley in 1986 and meets once a month. There is a membership of over 30 people interested in making their own wine as well as tasting commercially available wine. This is so popular that people travel from other villages to take part!

Membership of the **North Beds Theatre Club** has declined from its peak of over 100, but remains active. The club organises theatre trips to London, Cambridge, Northampton and now the new theatre at Milton Keynes.

Every summer there is a **Village Fete** with stalls and other attractions. The proceeds go to worthy causes within the village. The church also holds a fete in the vicarage garden.

**Ross Meadow** is a successful recent development of the ground between Church Lane and the brook. For many years this two acre plot was owned by the Ross family in Thurleigh and rented out for a variety of uses – keeping chickens, pasture for horses and market gardening.

At one time the meadow was filled with allotments, where villagers grew vegetables, fruit and flowers. Demand for the allotments dwindled and the area became untidy and underused.

In 1995, the Parish Council purchased the land for the use of villagers, ensuring that it was not used for housing development. With the help of a grant and a lot of hard work from a team of volunteers, ably led by Sheila and Tim Copping, the area has been turned into an attractive pocket park. There are seats amongst the trees, shrubs and flowers, so that villagers can stroll or sit to enjoy the plants and wildlife.

*Ross Meadow*

Ross Meadow seemed to the Women's Institute to be the most appropriate place to bury their Millennium Time Capsule. Early in the year 2000, Florence Wilkinson lowered the capsule into the ground where it will stay until the end of the 21st century. None of us will see it opened, but we hope that those who do will find the history within as interesting as everything we have uncovered of the past centuries. Perhaps they might even write a book ...

# Afterword

The committee of the Riseley Historical Society has greatly enjoyed researching and producing this book. We hope that it will provide an interesting record of life in Riseley in the latter part of the last millennium. Although there were many parties in Riseley on 31 December 1999, there was no 'village party' to celebrate the turn of the millennium. This book, however, a truly collaborative and co-operative effort involving many villagers, is a celebration.

We are aware that we have not been able to research or include everything that has and does go on. We apologise for any omissions or errors and would encourage anyone who feels they have information or a story to tell to contact the Riseley Historical Society, so that the information may be recorded and possibly included in a future publication.

Riseley is a flourishing village community – home to over 1200 adults and children. We now have only one village store and two public houses, but two successful schools and a variety of enterprises in and around the village.

Riseley still provides a lot of its own entertainment and some employment. People can participate in various village activities, but those who prefer a more private existence are respected. Residents born and raised here mingle happily with more recent arrivals, who bring different experiences and expertise to enrich village life.

Our village has been and is a good place to live – long may this continue.

## The Contributors

"Riseley – Our Village" has involved many of the villagers of Riseley – past and present. We have received help, information and support from current and previous residents. We regret that we cannot mention them all by name – another book would be required! Nevertheless, our heartfelt thanks to them all.

Many fascinating and lovely photographs have been lent to us. Some have been included in this book, others have been scanned and recorded to help to make the record of life in Riseley, which it is our aim to achieve. We have ambitions to create a website, which will allow access to the mass of information – photographic and otherwise, which we have accumulated. Again, our thanks to those who have entrusted us with treasured family photographs and shared this history with us.

Kevin Ward and the staff at Bedford County Record Office have provided invaluable help, advice and information. Bedford Reference Library and Marylebone Cricket Club have assisted by furnishing important information towards the construction of this book – our thanks to them also.

Three people have helped us specifically by word processing the text of this book. Marjorie Bosman, Mary Shiers and Sheila Gibson have pounded the keyboard and turned our authors' pearls of wisdom into readable text! Cheryl Goddard spent many hours proof reading the book and introducing consistency of style.

Sandra Walker and her pupils at the Margaret Beaufort School made a helpful contribution to the design of the book cover. Richard Harries worked on the drawing up of some of the maps inside the front cover and in the body of the book.

John Ashworth provided the Foreword for "Riseley – Our Village". He was a frequent visitor to Riseley in his early years. At one time John was Director of the London School of Economics. Currently he is Chairman of the Board of the British Library.

Keith Burgess and his team at Newnorth Print have given generously of their skill and expertise during the development of this project. They have also exhibited considerable patience and been endlessly supportive!

The committee of Riseley Historical Society have worked hard for two years on various aspects – research, fundraising, interviewing, collecting information and writing. Each has made a significant contribution and without their determination, teamwork and dedication, you would not be reading these words.

**Mike Ives**, chairman of the committee and the inspiration behind this book. He worked tirelessly to motivate the authors and to raise the funding necessary for this project.

*'Originally from Essex, my wife and I moved to Riseley in the early 1970s with our four children. They attended the lower and middle schools and were among the first pupils to attend Sharnbrook Upper School. Both Pat and I found many new friends and through the many organisations within the village began to take an active interest in village life. The best thing is when the children refer to Riseley as "home".'*

**Sue Davies**, editor, has put the book together, using the individual contributions from the various authors to create the finished article.

Sue has lived in Riseley since 1971. She taught at Keysoe County Primary School for a few years before leaving to have her own family. Sue and her husband George have lived in five different houses in the High Street, and their two boys attended Riseley Lower School and Margaret Beaufort before moving on the Sharnbrook Upper School. Sue has served on the PTAs and Governing Bodies of both village schools.

**Andrew Gell** – author of A Clearing in the Brushwood, Earning a Living, Hostelries and Public Houses and co-author of Sport, Parades and Village Events.

Andrew was born in the village, in the house where he lives now. He was educated solely in the village schools. His family – both on his father's and mother's side (Rootham) – have lived in the village for many hundreds of years. Andrew participates in many village organisations and activities and is currently chairman of the Parish Council.

**Julia Jarman** – author of The Village School.

Julia has lived in the village for over 25 years, with her husband and three children. She taught in local schools before becoming a writer of books for children.

**Barbara Jones** has helped with the collection of information for this book and carried out many of the interviews with villagers, past and present.

Barbara moved into Riseley on her marriage 34 years ago. A wife, mother of two sons, teacher and active co-owner of Brook House; she has also been involved in many village activities, particularly the village hall at its outset and more recently, on or behind stage with Riseley Drama Group productions.

**Colin Jones** has collected, scanned and indexed the many photographs connected with this project and the history of Riseley.

Colin has lived in the village for 34 years with his wife Barbara. During this time he has made a hobby of compiling a photographic record of the changes taking place in the village, right up to the present day. Some of these photographs are included in the computer scanned images used in this book.

**Phillip Nicholls** – author of All Saints Church and Moravians Methodists and Baptists.

Phillip has lived in Riseley for over 50 years. In 1982 he was licensed as a Church of England Lay Reader and has served on the Parochial Church Council for many years. He is very interested in church history.

**Peter Smith** – author of In Times of War and co-author of Sport, Parades and Village Events.

Peter came to Riseley with his wife Maureen in 1994. He and Maureen share an interest in family history and enjoy travelling in England in pursuit of this hobby.

**William Wallis** – author of Farming in Riseley.

William lives at Lodge Farm with his wife Lynne and their three children – Emma, Tom and Miriam. He is the third generation of his family to farm there, but the fifth generation to farm in Riseley on his mother's side. He was born in '*Invicta House*' on Riseley High Street and except for the time spent away at agricultural college, has lived in Riseley all his life.

**Florence Wilkinson** – author of Famous Faces and Our Village.

Florence came to Riseley with her husband Frank and two young sons in 1956. She worked in the sub post office for 13 years until 1977. Florence served on the Parish Council for many years and was president of the WI for 10 years. A founding member of the Village Hall Committee, she remains active in and committed to community life. She has always been interested in local history, particularly the history of Riseley.

# Bibliography

150 Years of Riseley VA Lower School – Judy Ruff
A History of RAE Bedford – Arthur Pearcy
Agriculture in Bedfordshire and Huntingdonshire
Bedfordshire Farm Worker in the 19th Century – Nigel E Agar
Bedfordshire Muster Lists – Nigel Lutt
Captain Swing – George Rude and E J Hobsbaum
History of Bedfordshire – Joyce Godber
Hit Hard and Enjoy It – Thomas Carter (Dickie) Dodds
Kelly's Directory 1898
Longbow – Robert Hardy
Medieval Warfare – Timothy Newark
Picture Post Magazine
Riseley and its Conservation Area – North Bedfordshire Borough Council
Riseley and its Conservation Area – printed and published by North Bedfordshire Borough Council
Riseley Primary School and the 1870 Education Act – Gillian K Shaw
The Domesday Book (Courtesy of Sharnbrook Community College)
The Ring of Roothams – Thelma Smith
The Victorian Country Child – Pamela Horn
The Victorian History of the Counties of England
Victoria County History for Bedfordshire

## Sponsors

Sponsorship has been received from the following organisations and individuals. Their generosity has made this publication possible.

Bedford Borough Council
Bedford Council for Voluntary Services
Bedfordshire County Council
Bedford Rural Communities Charity
Heritage Lottery Fund
Simon Whitbread Trust

G Davies
I Fitzgerald
A Gell
P Strickland